Lingering Human Spirits
Volume 2

Unravelling More of the Mystery

By

Dr. Ron M. Horner

Lingering Human Spirits
Volume 2

Unravelling More of the Mystery

By
Dr. Ron M. Horner

LifeSpring International Ministries
PO Box 5847
Pinehurst, North Carolina 28374
www.RonHorner.com

Lingering Human Spirits – Volume 2

Unraveling More of the Mystery

Dr. Ron M. Horner

Copyright ©2022 LifeSpring International Ministries, Inc.

Scripture is taken from the New King James Version®. Copyright © 1982 by Thomas Nelson. Used by permission. All rights reserved. (Unless otherwise noted.)

Scripture quotations marked (TPT) are from The Passion Translation®, Copyright © 2017, 2018 by BroadStreet Publishing Group, LLC. Used by permission. All rights reserved. ThePassionTranslation.com

Any trademarks mentioned are the property of their respective owners.

All rights reserved. This book is protected by the copyright laws of the United States of America. This book may not be copied or reprinted for commercial gain or profit. The use of short quotations or occasional page copying for personal, or group study is permitted and encouraged. Permission will be granted upon request.

Requests for bulk sales discounts, editorial permissions, or other information should be addressed to:

LifeSpring Publishing
PO Box 5847
Pinehurst, NC 28374 USA

Additional copies available at www.courtsofheaven.net

ISBN 13 TP: 978-1-953684-28-8
ISBN 13 eBook: 978-1-953684-29-5

Cover Design by Darian Horner Design
(www.darianhorner.com)
Images: stock.adobe.com: #229190440, #271554349, #311210871

First Edition: July 2022

10 9 8 7 6 5 4 3 2

Printed in the United States of America

Table of Contents

Acknowledgements i
Preface iii
Chapter 1 Heaven is Speaking, Are we Listening? 1
Chapter 2 What Happens When We Die? 7
Chapter 3 Conducting an LHS Check 21
Chapter 4 The Spreadsheet 33
Chapter 5 Blended Lingering Spirits 41
Chapter 6 Gathering Tares 47
Chapter 7 The Guest Registry 55
Chapter 8 Spirit Fragmentation 67
Chapter 9 Soul Fragmentation 73
Chapter 10 Body Fragmentation 91
Chapter 11 If You Build It, They Will Come 97
Chapter 12 Recognizing the Person 101
Chapter 13 Red & Black Capture Bags 105
Chapter 14 Silver & Gold Capture Bags 111
Chapter 15 Purple Capture Bags 125
Chapter 16 Green & Blue Capture Bags 127
Chapter 17 Orange, Brown & Tan Capture Bags 139

Chapter 18 Pink Capture Bags 153

Chapter 19 Unweaving Domains 165

Chapter 20 The Banners of the Lord............................. 171

Chapter 21 Overcoming the Familial Spirit................. 183

Chapter 22 Migrating LHS's & Double Dipping........... 197

Chapter 23 Speaking from the Grave............................ 205

Chapter 24 Testimony of Freedom................................ 209

Chapter 25 Conclusion.. 213

Appendix 215

Frequently Asked Questions 215

Accessing the Realms of Heaven................................... 221

Evil Timelines... 227

Description 243

About the Author 245

Other Books by Dr. Ron M. Horner............................... 247

Acknowledgements

This book is a compilation of engagements with Heaven and conversations with others who have begun to explore the world with lingering human spirits as part of the paradigm of the spiritual walk. My Executive Assistants have been very helpful in engagements with Heaven for revelation. I thank you ladies for your assistance.

Thank you, Anna Horan, for your editorial assistance. Thanks to all who contributed their stories, testimonies, and insights for this book. May we see multitudes enter their destiny in Heaven.

Preface

Since writing the first volume of this series two years ago, we have witnessed the freedom of multiplied thousands of lingering human spirits as they have been assisted in transitioning to Heaven. In the process we have had our eyes opened to additional insights and revelations that will prove beneficial to you as you read this book. If you have not read the first book, you need to stop where you are and go back and read the first volume, *Lingering Human Spirits*.[1] This book will not make sense to you otherwise.

This book is to assist those who have already embraced this concept that was introduced by Jesus in Matthew and Luke, so it is not a new concept, simply an unveiled one. You may recall that the experience of the Baptism in the Holy Spirit with the evidence of speaking in tongues was lost from the church for many centuries and only in the early 1900's did the church experience a

---

[1] *Lingering Human Spirits* by Dr. Ron M. Horner, (LifeSpring Publishing) 2020. Available at www.courtsofheaven.net.

revisitation of that dynamic experience. Now the Pentecostal/charismatic stream of Christianity is the fastest growing stream in Christendom. Just because we are not familiar with something does not mean that it is not true, truth, or present-day reality.

In this volume you will read of testimonies of those ministering to lingering human spirits (LHS's) or even remembrances from the LHS themselves. These are quite remarkable.

If you have ever wondered about the condition of our society, especially the prevailing darkness over many of our cities, and wondered why, then the concept of lingering human spirits will broaden your understanding of how so much darkness is prevailing. It is not just demons but LHS's on assignment by darkness. Remember, that Satan only has a limited number of demons, and a lot of people exist on the planet. He needs more workers, and so he hijacks (for lack of a better description) human spirits who have not transitioned into Heaven or Hell. They are given assignments of evil to plague humanity with. The first volume taught you how to deal with these situations and how to get these human spirits freed from their demonic assignment as well as the evil power acting as the boss over the demons involved. Freedom is simple. It generally involves repentance, then dealing from the top down with the boss, dealing with the demonic guard(s), and finally addressing the lingering human spirit to help them transition to their eternal destiny where they stand before the Father and request mercy to be shown them.

Or, if they are not interested in Heaven, they do have an alternative destiny, albeit not a nice one—hell.

We will also discuss some of the many reasons LHS's don't make the transition. Some of the reasons will be eye-opening to you. We must realize that most preaching about Heaven has painted a poor picture of the beauty and glory of Heaven, therefore many people are not excited about Heaven as an eternal option. They don't want to play a harp for ten thousand years. Neither do I.

Heaven has a lot more in store than long worship services, clouds, cutesy angelic beings, and gold streets. It is another realm of existence that few have truly comprehended. Much of our preaching has also been focused on Heaven as an eternal destiny only available if you died, but no! We can experience the Glory of Heaven now.

As you read these pages, do so with your spirit forward and your soul at rest. This book contains revelation and insight, and these things can only truly be grasped by your spirit—not your soul. Let your spirit feed on this material. Ask Holy Spirit to teach you and fill in the blanks on questions you might have as you read. Then, help more lingering human spirits to freedom in the realm of Heaven. They await our assistance.

Now for those of you who haven't read the first book, but would like a brief explanation of the concept of Lingering Human Spirits, here it is:

A Short Explanation of LHS's

Recently someone asked me about this subject as they had been told I had said something I did not say. I try to be very careful with what I say and some words I simply do not use to minimize the confusion. However, just like the children's game where one person whispers something in the ear of the person beside them, and that person does the same to the person beside them until it goes around the entire room—invariably, what is heard by the last person was nowhere close to what had been originally said. The following is a brief explanation about LHS's that you might find useful. This is what I wrote:

> *I thought I would try to clear up your concerns about what I refer to as lingering human spirits that we dealt with in your session. The verse[2] you mentioned is not doctrine and doesn't include or exclude a time frame in-between the two events— dying and judgment. Nor is the verse to be absent from the body is to be present from the Lord[3]— that was Paul's anticipation. As a believer they can expect to move immediately into Heaven, but not all who die are ready to begin eternity and are hesitant to begin, therefore the spirit wanders around seeking rest or a resting place. The unbelieving spirit certainly doesn't want to step*

---

[2] Hebrews 9:27 And as it is appointed for men to die once, but after this the judgment.

[3] 2 Corinthians 5:8

into their eternity and will do everything in their power to remain, even if it involves wandering in the waterless place. Those who die in battle may be resolved to die but are usually hoping to not die. Those whose death is by murder or genocide were not desiring to die, but it was forced upon their bodies. These spirits wander seeking rest as Jesus spoke of in Matthew 12:43-45 (also in Luke 11). Understand that the use of the word "unclean spirit" was to differentiate between them and the Holy Spirit. It also was a reference to the spirit being ceremonially unclean based on Jewish tradition. The Jews had an entire process for preparation for burial (remember the death of Jesus and the women that brought spices to prepare Jesus' body for burial).

The Matthew 12 passage of Scripture was poorly translated which is partially why we always thought it was talking about demons. Unclean spirits are not demons. Revelation 18:3 points this out as well. There is more to be said but this should summarize it for you. To have a lingering human spirit is not typically some evil thing; they were simply looking for a body to live out their destiny in and since their body was no longer available, they hitched a ride with you. That is especially common when babies die—they do not want to leave mama. Releasing them to Heaven is a simple thing. They have a destiny in Heaven too! You are just helping them begin it.

Chapter 1

Heaven is Speaking, Are we Listening?

Heaven will often use the media of this world to get ideas and concepts to us. However, often we are not disposed to even consider that maybe God is trying to show us something.

Think of all the movies that have touched on this subject in some fashion or other. We can hardly use these movies for their theological accuracy (because we probably won't find any), but many time the Father is trying to get a concept to us and movies are one of the best ways to do it.

Think of a few examples:

Ugetsu (1953)

Always (1989)

Ghost (1990)

The Sixth Sense (1999)

The Others (2001)

Pulse (2001)

Personal Shopper (2016)

Ghostbusters I, II, III

et.al.

Heaven has tried to acquaint us with the idea for a long time, but we are sometimes slow to take the hint. The New Age movement has had some understanding of the concept, but they have no redemptive result. We have seen an influx of Zombie movies that pervert the concept and try to induce fear into lives instead of the hope the the Body of Christ can bring into the picture.

The Body of Christ has been slow to pick up on many concepts that the world has been more ready to embrace and that is to our chagrin. Because of the abdication of responsibilities of the Body of Christ, the world and the realms of darkness have readily stepped in to introduce a perverted concept of many ideals. The redemptive work that is the ministry to lingering spirits is one of those.

Consider all those who were believers and had lived lives faithful to God who have passed from this earth realm into the dry places that Jesus spoke of in Matthew 12 and are seeking rest. They are caught between time and eternity and not until recent years has help been available to them through the ministry of Arthur Burk and others. Few have been willing to press the boundaries of social and religious tradition to work to transition those who are ready to begin their eternal destiny in Heaven. Most people do not understand that they not only have a destiny on earth, but also have one in Heaven. When we die we do not cease to exist, we simply cease to have an earth suit. The moment we choose to believe in Jesus and accept His sacrifice on our behalf, we begin our never-ending existence as an eternal spirit living the *zoe* life of God, whether on earth on in Heaven. Our eternal life doesn't start when our body dies, we have already started it. The only difference is the realm we live it in.

Someone I know who has lived their life in faithfulness to God and now their body is winding down admitted to my wife that she, although a believer in Jesus, who formerly served as a pastor's wife, is afraid to die. She has heard sermon after sermon about someone's interpretation of Heaven—streets of gold and all that—but after more than 60 years as a believer, is not sure about Heaven. That is a tragedy. It is unnecessary for her to suffer as her body is shutting down when the hope that is before her will make her wonder, once she does finally transition into Heaven—why did I take so long?

Think of the benefit of helping just the believers whose body died to make the transition to their eternal destiny in Heaven. Currently these lingering persons are trying to get our attention through various physical manifestations either to our body or to our realms and we have not taken the hint. Therefore, they linger, unable to fulfill their destiny in Heaven.

Over and over again, lingering spirits we have ministered to have told us they are tired and just want to go home. This coincides with what Jesus said about them wandering about seeking rest (see Matthew 12).

Then we have those who, although not a believer when their body died, are not anti-God, they just never accepted Jesus in their life on earth. Many, even in Western cultures, know nothing of the real Jesus. Churches are simply museums of irrelevance to them. What if, by ministering to them when they come near our realms, they are ushered through the silver channel and stand before the Father requesting mercy? What if mercy meets them and they spend the rest of their existence in Heaven? Would that not be wonderful? Remember, the Father wants to populate Heaven, not hell!

To minister to lingering spirits in this manner will require that we let go of some old assumptions that we have held dear and consider that if a lingering spirit has not reached Heaven, the Father is still reaching out to them—even after their body has died. We get to help in their final transition into Heaven. They don't have to stay in the desert place, the can enjoy the refreshing of Heaven.

Then we have those lingering spirits that have been captured by forces of darkness and made to do their bidding. Even though they have been captivated by a demonic guard, most do not want to be in servitude to demons. If we have embraced what we have shared in my book *Lingering Human Spirits: Unraveling the Mystery*, then we know how to bring them to freedom and shut down that demonic outlet that has been wreaking havoc in someone's life.

As a lingering spirit who was under the domination of a demonic guard told a colleague, they did not want to hurt the person they were assigned to. They were forced to harm them. They did it under duress. We understand that is more than likely the common thought—they were forced to serve the demonic forces because most people are not inherently evil. The want to do good things but sometimes need to be pointed in the right direction.

In 2 Peter 3:9, we read:

This means that, contrary to man's perspective, the Lord is not late with his promise to return, as some measure lateness. But rather, His "delay" simply reveals His loving patience toward you, because **He does not want any to perish but all to come to repentance.** *(TPT) (Emphasis mine)*

The aim of the Father is to bring all men to repentance. He did not limit the time frame as we have been taught to believe. Just as our enemy will try to force someone (while a lingering spirit) to torment another person, Satan continues his activities after a person passes from this life. Why should the Father not be able to do the same?

As we read this book we have expanded our understanding of how to assist lingering spirits and we have learned ways to assist in the mass transition of large groups of LHS's. As mentioned in the prior book, I have been involved in aiding the transition of masses of people caught in shipwrecks, airline crashes, industrial tragedies, those lost in battle, and more. The opportunities are endless. May we be about the Father's business and help these wandering ones to find home.

———·———

Chapter 2

What Happens When We Die?

For those who are reading this book anyway without having read the first volume, let me take a few pages and introduce the concept. Some of this is taken from the first volume, but will also serve as a short refresher course on the topic.

In the evangelical church tradition I was raised in, we were taught that immediately upon death we went to stand before God and awoke for judgment once the rapture had occurred. We have two Scriptures that are sacred to that belief system:

> *And as it is appointed for men to die once, but after this the judgment."* (Hebrews 9:27)

> *So, we are always confident, knowing that while we are at home in the body, we are absent from the Lord. ⁷ For we walk by faith, not by sight. ⁸ We are confident, yes, well pleased **rather to be***

> ***absent from the body and to be present with the Lord.*** *⁹ Therefore we make it our aim, whether present or absent, to be well pleasing to Him. ¹⁰ For we must all appear before the judgment seat of Christ, that each one may receive the things done in the body, according to what he has done, whether good or bad. (2 Corinthians 5:6-10) (Emphasis mine)*

We live with the assumption that between the time of death and our appearing before the judgment seat of Christ, no time elapses that we can discern. We assume:

> *Our body dies—our spirit immediately appears before God.*

In the process, we use these Scriptures to create doctrines when these oft-believed concepts are NOT doctrines. They are beliefs. They may even be commonly held beliefs, but still, they are not doctrines, nor can they be.

We also neglect the following Scripture so we can come to that conclusion:

> *When an unclean spirit goes out of a man, he goes through dry places, seeking rest, and finds none. (Matthew 12:43)*

These words of Jesus seem to challenge the immediacy concept we have generally believed. Jesus is speaking in the Matthew 12 passage, and He opens an entirely different possibility—one we have conveniently ignored because it did not fit our preconceptions. We have made several assumptions that we need to revisit.

In the first book in this series, I unpacked some things that are well outside our traditional box, but I am not alone. Others are beginning to see these concepts and make personal reconsiderations that have challenged what they have long believed. I reviewed every instance of the ministry of Jesus and noted the distinctions between (1) deliverance from demons and dealing with what the translators termed (2) "unclean spirits" and also (3) "evil spirits"—three different concepts.

In modern Christianity we have lumped all of them together, when only rarely in the New Testament were there instances of a disembodied spirit and a demon involved. I will use the term lingering human spirit (LHS) to describe a human spirit that is no longer in their original body but have yet to step into their eternity—whether Heaven or hell.

In the first Scripture mentioned,

> *And as it is appointed for men to die once, but after this the judgment. (Hebrews 9:27) (Emphasis mine)*

...this verse is expressing the perfect will and desired protocol of the Father. It is his desire that every person, when they die as a believer, would immediately stand before the Lord for "judgment" and be granted access into the realms of Heaven.

> *It helps us if we believe that God is not trying to populate Hell, but rather populate Heaven.*

The late Reinhard Bonnke wrote a book entitled *Plundering Hell to Populate Heaven*. Hell was not designed for us. It was designed for the devil and his angels. A person can go there if they want to, but it is not the top spot on the Eternity Tour.

As mentioned earlier, we cannot make a doctrine out of this verse. Particularly, considering Jesus' message in Matthew where it is recorded that He said,

> *When an unclean spirit goes out of a man, he goes through dry places, seeking rest, and finds none. (Matthew 12:43)*

If they are a Christian when they die, why don't they just enter Heaven immediately?

Much of our theology and understanding of Heaven and hell is so skewed that people are not as sure of their eternal future as they may want us to believe.

They may pass from this life only to find that they don't have to immediately transition.

Many who have called on the Lord have not lived lives pleasing to the Lord and therefore may not be sure of their destination.

Therefore, they wait.

For instance:

We were raised to believe we have an unconditional eternal security; however, we know that we have not lived righteously before God and therefore we are not so sure about what we were taught. Our conscience convicts us of sin, but we continue in a lifestyle of sin. Are we certain Heaven will take us like we are?

Or...

We were raised to believe we had NO security in our salvation—that it could be lost at any time.

When we pass, do we really know where we stand with God?

We are not in a hurry to find out!

Again, our doctrines have often created more uncertainty than security, even about Heaven and hell.

Reason 1: Uncertainty about Heaven

Jesus entirely left open the possibility that the spirit of a human following the death of their body may not always make the full transition into Heaven. We might say, "Well, why not?"

This is likely because of the dearth of accurate preaching about death, dying, and eternity. Most of us have had little accurate preaching about these things and much of what we heard was so full of fear that we weren't sure if we were going to make it into Heaven when we died or even if we wanted to go.

Some time back a friend of many years passed away from cancer. Upon hearing of his passing, I and a seer checked to see if he had transitioned. I had led him to Jesus years before but had limited contact with him in the last few years.

We found he had not transitioned and was very puzzled as to where he was. He kept repeating how he needed to get back to his work calendar because he had a lot of work to do. We explained to him that his body had died and that he needed to transition into his eternal destiny. He said, "You mean Heaven isn't all clouds and fluffy stuff?" We assured him that Heaven was not as he had envisioned. With this comfort, we opened the silver channel and angels assisted him to stand before the Father, where we recommended that he simply call out for mercy to the Father when he got there so that he would have entrance into Heaven.

His only exposure to church had been in a conservative denomination where they talked a lot about getting saved but did not teach very accurately about Heaven. He wasn't sure Heaven was all that great of a place to go to.

Reason 2: Not Sure I Qualify

Were it not for the mercy of God, none of us would "qualify" for Heaven. However, God, in His mercy through the sacrifice of Jesus, made it possible for us to enter Heaven. His work qualifies us. We simply accept it in our behalf and receive it.

When ministering to an LHS, it may be necessary to explain this to them and assure them that God is not opposed to them, rather He is deeply in love with them and wants to spend an eternity with them.

Often, we will need to patiently and lovingly reason with an LHS who has questions. However, don't get bogged down in answering question after question. Simply explain to them that they need to reserve those questions for the Father himself to answer when they stand before Him. Don't let them badger us with endless questions.

Reason 3: I'm Not Allowed to Go

A recent experience related to me is an example of the falsehoods many have heard about Heaven.

> *I had to go to our farm to take care of some things and while at the farm I asked Holy Spirit if there were any LHS's at the fire pit. I heard three. I asked them their names and got James, John, and Matthew. I asked them "Why are you here?" and they stated that they knew I was coming to the farm. I asked, "Why did you not go on [to Heaven when they died]", and heard, "We are not allowed to go."*

I asked, "What do you mean you are not allowed to go?" They stated, "We could not go because we are not Baptized in the Holy Ghost." I told them that was a lie and that they could go. I told them that their angels were there and would take them through the Silver Channel to Jesus. I opened the Silver Channel and sent them on their way to Jesus.

A similar scenario may happen with those of the Catholic faith who died without receiving the Last Rites administered by a priest. In the teaching as many understand it, they cannot enter Heaven not having partaken of the sacraments.

We have found that we ask angels to provide someone to administer the Eucharist to them prior to opening the silver channel. We acknowledge their concern and note that Heaven has provided for that via an angel to administer the Eucharist to them. Typically, they are happy to transition through the silver channel at that point.

Reason 4: Fear of Judgment

Many have heard teaching that tells them that immediately upon death they are going to stand before God and be judged for their sins, but is that accurate?

They use this Scripture:

And as it is appointed for men to die once, but after this the judgment [justice]. (Hebrews 9:27)

We assume that once someone dies, immediately they will experience judgment, however the context clearly says something different than what we have understood.

*²²And according to the law almost all things are purified with blood, and without shedding of blood there is no remission. ²³ Therefore it was necessary that the copies of the things in the heavens should be purified with these, but the heavenly things themselves with better sacrifices than these. ²⁴ For Christ has not entered the holy places made with hands, which are copies of the true, but into Heaven itself, now to appear in the presence of God for us; ²⁵ not that He should offer Himself often, as the high priest enters the Most Holy Place every year with blood of another— ²⁶ He then would have had to suffer often since the foundation of the world; but now, once at the end of the ages, **He has appeared to put away sin by the sacrifice of Himself**.*

*²⁷ And as it is appointed for men to die once, but after this the judgment, ²⁸ so **Christ was offered once to bear the sins of many**. To those who eagerly wait for Him He will appear a second time, apart from sin, for salvation. (Emphases mine) (Hebrews 9:22-28)*

This passage tells us that Jesus, at the crucifixion, already bore the penalty (the judgment) for all our sins and mine, as well as for those of the whole world. Our sins have already been judged. Verse 27 says that it is appointed to men once to die but after this the justice—that is a better translation for that verse. We are standing before God to be judged for our sins—they have already been judged.

Romans 4:7-8 reads:

7 Blessed are those whose lawless deeds are forgiven, and whose sins are covered; 8 blessed is the man to who the Lord shall not impute sin.

The writer of Hebrews wrote in Hebrews 10:17:

...then He adds, 'their sins and lawless deeds I will remember no more.'

We don't have to be afraid when we stand before God! If we are, simply call upon His mercy. Remember, He wants to fill up Heaven. It has no membership quota! He is not trying to fill up hell! If we have called upon Jesus to save us, He will.

We will be rewarded for our deeds[4] so we want to be sure our deeds are pleasing to the Father. That passage indicates it is good news for those who work good and not so good news for those whose works are evil.

---

[4] Romans 1:1-11

The justice of God would demand that we not be penalized for something already taken care of. We can depend on the mercy of God to be His first response toward us.

Reason 5: Suicide

Many have been taught that suicide was, in effect, an unpardonable sin and therefore an automatic ticket to hell. This creates the belief, "I can't be received into Heaven." If their upbringing was Catholic and someone committed suicide, they were denied the right of a "Christian" burial. However, I would ask the question. When someone commits suicide, are they at that point in their right mind? Are they likely under a tremendous amount of duress? Do we think the mercy of God would be extended to them in that situation?

Since our Father is a God of mercy, He is likely more merciful than we consider. Samson, who died when he collapsed the palace, was also listed in the Hall of Faith of Hebrews 11. Was not his death technically a suicide? And if it was, how was he listed for his example of faith along with Enoch and Abraham? I submit to us that the mercy of God may well be available to those who in that state, end their life.

How do LHS's find me?

Some who have worked with transitioning LHS's have inquired as to how they heard about them. Here are a few of the reasons we have heard:

1. **My angel told me to come here.** This is common to those who have worked to help LHS's transition to Heaven. Angels will attempt to send an LHS to where the LHS can receive help. Sometimes, angels bring them to someone who knows how to assist them.
2. **We heard it on YouTube.** Once they hear about someone who can help, they will find their way to them for assistance. Others may not have heard about it on YouTube (or something similar) but have heard about it in the atmosphere where they are.
3. **I saw the light in you** and knew you could help me. We have heard this reason multiple times.
4. **You were peaceful. I knew you were a safe place.** LHS's are drawn to those who are peaceful for the feel they will provide a safe habitation until their transition.
5. **I was told you would be able to help me someday.** This is a curious response because it indicates that somehow their spirit had a knowing that one day you would come into this revelation and would be able to help them transition to Heaven.

Although these are just a few of the reasons LHS's find people, I am sure a myriad of other reasons exists. It is not a bad thing when an LHS finds us (if they don't have a demonic guard). They are simply wanting to go home, and we will be able to help them. Follow the steps in this book and we will be able to participate in this redemptive work of the cross.

Even if they have a demonic guard, they are usually not serving that guard willingly but under duress. Those lingering spirits simply want to go home as well and be freed from the domination of the demonic guard and their boss(es).

Chapter 3

Conducting an LHS Check

As my co-worker and I were working with a client and wanted to check for Lingering Human Spirit (LHS) activity. We stepped into Heaven and requested access to the Guest Registry office and asked to see the Guest Registry for Mark.[5] Looking at the Guest Registry, a woman named Harriet was seen as well as an army veteran named Joseph.

We looked at the Guest Registry, and then investigated the realm where they were to address them. In the Guest Registry it also noted which realm they were in within Mark's body.

A Hispanic man named Jesús and a woman named Harriet were listed. We asked the attendant where these LHS's were lodged in Mark's body realm.

---

[5] Name has been changed.

One LHS was simply hanging around Mark's realm, while the other was picked up at a hotel where Mark had stayed.

Mark had just finished a stay at a hotel a few days prior. An LHS named Joseph was also listed who was picked up at the airport where Mark had also been. He, too, was simply hanging around, but in his case, he was on an assignment. Information continued to be gained on Joseph who died through depression and complications of pharmacopoeia (drug use). He did not step into Heaven because he was angry that he did not get to fulfill the purpose he thought he would fulfill, and he was still carrying that anger. The reason he did not fulfill it was because of his soul's emotions. These soul emotions caused him to fall under the deception of medications, and he was mad about that.

We asked, "What about Jesús? Why can't I find any information about Jesús? Why does that suddenly seem to go blank? What question should I ask to find out more about Jesús?"

We decided to ask for information about "Time of Entry" for Jesús by asking, "When did he enter Mark's realm?"

In response we began to know of a time when Mark was on an airplane flying to another country and the time frame when this occurred—three years ago. Jesús came into Mark's realm while he was in the Miami airport. He was on an assignment of the Kundalini spirit to torment Mark physically. We could also detect where

Jesús was in Mark's physical realm—in his lower back. During Jesús' life, he had defied God, so when he died, he did not want to enter hell but agreed to be assigned by the demonic boss, the Kundalini spirit, and was assigned to torment Mark. Specifically, his assignment was to torment officers in the army of God.

An additional note was in the registry that indicated Mark had fallen while on that trip.

Somewhat surprised, Mark acknowledged that he had fallen in the shower shortly after arriving at the hotel where he stayed. In the fall he injured a finger. The details even indicated the color of the shower stall he had fallen in. The phrase "Inflicted Damages" was listed in one of the columns.

The Guest Registry is a source of a tremendous amount of information, much more than we imagined. We can read from the registry, or ask an attendant, or Holy Spirit to read to us the contents of what we are searching for, or assist us to perceive the information.

Since the client had suffered "Inflicted Damages," restitution can be sought from the Court of Reclamations.

Of the three LHS's in Mark's realms, Jesús has been in his realms the longest. Harriet had simply found Mark as she had been lost and wandering about. Joseph did not make the transition into Heaven due to his anger at the ending of his life on earth. Joseph did not have a demonic guard, only unresolved anger. Both Harriet and Joseph were in Mark's overall sphere and not in a particular realm. Jesús, however, was in Mark's body realm and had been operating from that place during his stay.

Although this sleuthing seemed to be taking a long time, we were learning things we had not been aware of before. I had forgotten about how LHS's can sometimes lodge in a part of someone's body. It was important to know, specifically, in this situation. Holy Spirit had brought that to our remembrance.

As we discussed what we were learning, it also was revealed that if we feel we are being watched all the time, that it may be an LHS on assignment who, while lingering in our realms, reports on us to his demonic boss. We realized that we had dealt with an LHS on assignment a few weeks prior who was referred to as a "snitch."

At this point, our angels were called near, and we asked Holy Spirit to help the lingering human spirits around Mark's realms were called to come forth.

We have found when dealing with LHS's that some do not want to come forth out of fear of another LHS or fear of a demon (particularly some demonic bosses).

We may need to ask angels to go round them up and bring them forth. Specifically, we asked the angels to bring Harriet, Joseph, and Jesús out to where she could see them, regardless of where they had been abiding.

Speaking to Jesús, we instructed the LHS, saying, "I am speaking to you in the name of Jesus Christ. You are trespassing. You have no legal right to remain where you have been in Mark's lower spine. Angels, I ask that you go and round up the demonic guard that has been enforcing Jesús's assignment." When the demon was brought forth, it was requested that the angels put the demon in gold chains and gag him.[6]

Perceiving a demon in the mix, we inquired and asked Jesús if this demon was his tormentor to which he replied, "Yes." Jesús began calling out, "Don't send me anywhere else! Don't send me anywhere else!"

The demon was told, "Well, we *are* going to send you someplace else, and you are going to have to work that out with the Father." Next, we dealt with the boss of the demonic guard—the Kundalini spirit. Not rushing to simply cast the Kundalini spirit out, only to have it possibly return later, we wanted to know what gave it a right to be there?

Immediately we heard, "Mark's mom's fear of him traveling, his mom's fear of the demonic, and her fear of witchcraft (which seemed to be the primary one)." We had the sense that Mark's mom had spoken of this fear, knowingly or unknowingly. She was afraid of him coming under witchcraft while he traveled.

---

[6] We have found it helpful many times to have the angels bind the demons with gold chains and to put a muzzle on their mouth as they often are very annoying with what they say and often will curse and blaspheme.

Father, I request access to appear in your Mercy Court on behalf of Mark and on behalf of his mother who uttered words of fear regarding Mark's travel.

I repent on behalf of Mark's mom for her alignment and agreement with the fear of witchcraft. I confess this as sin where she saw witchcraft bigger than God; evil spirits bigger than the power of the Kingdom of God and the power of the Holy Spirit; and where she agreed with fear, where she agreed with the lie of fear, where she spoke fearful thoughts, where she believed something bad would happen, whether knowingly or unknowingly. I confess that as sin against a holy God, and I request Father that as you hear my repentance on her behalf, that this sin would come under the blood of Jesus. Yes, I specifically repent on behalf of Mark's mom for agreement for the fear of witchcraft. I ask that Your blood would cover her fear. I bless her, I release her, and I forgive her in Your name, Jesus.

Inquiring of Holy Spirit if any other thing that would give the Kundalini spirit access was still unresolved, nothing was brought to our attention, so we began,

I address the Kundalini spirit in the name of Jesus Christ. Your assignment against Mark is finished. It is over today. Your assignment against this lingering human spirit is finished and over today. I speak to the Kundalini spirit. You are a liar. You

are associated with the father of lies and nothing you say is true. I do not believe you because you cannot speak in truth. Therefore, this lingering human spirit is not yours. You do not own him. He is a human, and the Father is His maker and His creator; and it falls to the Father to be the judge, not you. I command you to flee in the name of Jesus and take your lies with you. I speak to Jesús in the spirit, in the name of Jesus. I know that you are there. You are going to be evicted today from Mark's lower spine.

I speak to the demonic guard. You are going to be taken to the feet of Jesus today. You have been overcome and overturned by a higher and superior court, by the blood of Jesus Christ. I am here releasing angels to cause you to flee now. Father, I ask that angels come and take this low-level demon to the feet of Jesus for processing.

Then speaking to the lingering human spirit, "Jesús, in the name of Jesus, your oppressor is gone, and the boss is gone. You have an opportunity. I am going to open the silver channel. Angels are going to come get you and you are going to go through it. You can go in chains, or you can go by them holding your hand, but you are going to leave Mark's lower spine now, in Jesus' name. When you get before the throne of God, the character of God is mercy. You will have an opportunity to request mercy. In the name of Jesus, I open the silver channel. Angels, come through the silver channel and take Jesús by the hand.

Jesús was reluctant to leave, so additional angels were requested. Speaking to Jesús, the seer said, "Yes, you are being forced to leave now. Go on through the silver channel."

Thank you, Father for those angels. All right. Jesús has gone through.

[The silver channel was then closed in the name of Jesus. Typically, when dealing with an LHS we will find spiritual debris in the host's realms.]

I ask that the spiritual debris would be cleansed from Mark's spine in his physical body—in this sphere of his physical body. I ask for angels to minister wholeness, healing, and alignment to the spine, in Jesus' name. I ask for the 'Amendment of The Sword of the Spirit' to excise anything that has been added to his DNA and to cauterize the DNA from any leakage in Jesus' name.

The other two LHS's had been watching this and so they were addressed as well:

I speak to Joseph in the name of Jesus Christ. Joseph, I am sorry for your life that it was cut short, that it was not lived in the quality that you had hoped it would be lived in. I am sorry for that. I commiserate with you that, that is unfortunate.

However, the news you do not know is that you still have a destiny. You have an opportunity to continue living as a spirit in God's Kingdom, the Kingdom of Jesus Christ. You are trespassing in Mark's realms, and I'm going to open the silver channel and an angel is going to come. I want you to go through the silver channel. You can ask the mercy of the Father when you get to the other side. Okay?

Speaking to Harriet, the seer said:

I speak to you in the name of Jesus Christ. You are trespassing in Mark's realms. I am sorry that your life ended so soon. I want to let you know that you still have a destiny in Heaven, and you will be able to see from His kingdom what your assignment is from there and what your family is doing from there. You will have greater opportunity to minister to them from Heaven. I am sorry for the unfortunate ending of your life, but your life is not over. You have opportunity to ask the Father's mercy and to move into His Kingdom through the silver channel, but no more wandering. Okay?

Father, in the name of Jesus, I open the silver channel. I ask for angels to come and take Joseph by the hand and lead him through. I ask angels to come and take Harriet and lead her through as well. Goodbye. And in the name of Jesus, I close the silver channel.

> *Father, I ask for angels to come and minister to Mark's realms. Clean up all spiritual debris left behind by lingering human spirits, smooth what has been wrinkled, straighten that which that which has been put into disorder or chaos. Let peace flow to Mark's realms in the name of Jesus. Cleanse any deposit of spiritual debris. Vacuum it up and dispose of it, in the name of Jesus.*

Often, we have found that after helping LHS's transition, we may find other LHS's who had stayed hidden during the process. They sometimes hide out of fear of another LHS or of a demonic guard or its boss. Once they see nothing evil happened to the LHS's that had been helped to transition, they are more likely to come forward. In one situation, a grandmotherly type hid until we had dealt with another LHS's demonic guards. Not only was she in hiding out of fear of the demonic guards, but she was also hiding several infants and small children that were in the clients' realms.

Early on in my understanding of the Guest Registry, I had been impressed to flip the pages of the registry to see if an entry had been made, but not made sequentially in the book, just like someone signing a register at a funeral might flip to another page and sign their name on another page and instead of signing right after the prior entry. As strange as that seems, I have seen it when I'm looking at the registry where they were not on the first page. They were on the second or third page although no entries were in-between.

———·———

Chapter 4

The Spreadsheet

Continuing the same series of engagements with Heaven, the attendant suggested we look at the registry like a spreadsheet. On a spreadsheet we can sort the data in a myriad of ways. The attendant suggested that we sort by Date of Entry, sort by Hiddenness, or even sort by Location (where in the hosts realms LHS might be—spirit realm, soul realm, or body realm; or even what body parts within the body realm). Essentially, find what room in the host's house are they located. We learned we could also sort by Realms (what realm they are currently in (body realm, soul realm, spirit realm, or another realm). Sometimes LHS's are not in a particular realm but in a person's sphere[7] of which the realms of body, soul, and spirit are a part—simply hanging out.

---

[7] One's sphere is comprised of the various realms of a person.

We realized that if she could see it like a spreadsheet, we could sort it and bring the information forward. The attendant explained that some are on assignment so we can sort by whether they are on Assignment. We can sort by hiddenness.

The attendant explained that a lingering human spirit who does not know God would want to stay hidden from our sight because he's comfortable where he's found a place. He has hidden himself there. As we are learning to discern them, we have seen the easy ones to see, and we are seeing them easier in the realm. We are discerning them when they are just around (in no particular realm). We are also discerning them when they are in the geographical location—the physical plane—where they are in the house. He told us that we were doing that and that we could in the future.

Some lingering human spirits have a vested interest in staying hidden. They are frightful of God. They are frightful of those who can operate like we are operating, and they are comfortable in their present state. We must point out them that they are trespassing, and they need to move on to begin their destiny in Heaven. Then help them in the process.

When we are sorting in Excel on a spreadsheet, we can do it by ascending order or descending order. Descending order would bring the oldest to the top, so, if sorting by the LHS's Date of Entry, it will sort by Date of Entry and bring the oldest entries to the top of the sort.

We requested to sort Mark's spreadsheet by descending order, meaning I see the oldest hidden one there, or if I want to sort by descending Date of Entry AND Hiddenness, I can. The attendant was very willing to assist us. We requested a sort by the longest duration, the most hidden lingering human spirit in Mark's Guest Registry. In way of the response, a vision was given where the seer saw someone who was believed to be an aunt—possibly a great aunt. Her name seemed to be Marjorie or Margaret. She died when Mark was around the age of seven and came to him when he was on a playground. It caused nightmares in Mark around this time. She simply did not want to die, but she did not know what was after death and she chose to stay. Heaven calls her ignorant. She was an aunt loosely related in the bloodline.

We needed to know where she was in Mark's realms. Sometimes if we are having trouble discerning remember the angelic weapon known as fog dispeller. TI does what its name implies. Simply ask for fog dispeller for our angels, then commission them for the use of the fog dispeller.

If we are unable to discern from the registry, we can also simply look in the realms of the person we are working on behalf of or in this situation were instructed by the attendant to have a scan done of Mark's body.

In the book on the Courts of Healing, I talk about different scans that can be done on a person. The attendant suggested we do a scan around Mark's body realm to determine the location of this LHS. We requested the scan and saw what appeared as a silhouette of Mark's body. The brain and one of the kidneys were highlighted. This indicated that the LHS was in Mark's physical realm.

Asking for angels to access Mark's physical realm and reveal the lingering human spirit. As soon that request was made the LHS went to the kidney. We asked the angels to get the LHS from the left kidney. We then spoke to the LHS saying, "You are trespassing. You cannot stay any longer. I speak to you in the name of Jesus."

Speaking to the angels, she requested that the angels get the LHS and hold her by the hands and bring her to where she could be seen.

Speaking again to the LHS, we said, "I am sorry for your loss of life. I am sorry that you did not know what to do—you were kind of clueless, but you cannot stay on earth. You cannot stay in this physical plane. You cannot stay in Mark's body. You are trespassing. You are going against the principles of God, who created you *and* Mark. You are going to be evicted. Now, you are going to go through the silver channel. When you get through the silver channel, you will see the Father, and you will have a conversation with Him. Ask Him for mercy."

In this situation we had no demonic guards to deal with, so we opened the silver channel and asked for angels to come and assist the LHS to transition into Heaven.

Upon the LHS's exit, we closed the silver channel in the name of Jesus. We then asked healing angels to come and cleaning angels to come, saying, "I ask for these angels to come and cleanse Mark's physical realm, especially of the left kidney. I ask that it be cleansed and purified. I ask Father, for Living Water to be placed there. I ask for the alignment of the DNA. I ask for the Amendment of the Sword of the Spirit and for an Amendment of 'As if it Never Were.' I ask for the purification and cleansing and bringing back to perfection the left kidney, in Jesus' name."

After thanking the Father, we asked to see the registry again for Mark. Looking at it as a spreadsheet, we asked to do a search by descending Date of Entry to see any other older, hidden lingering human spirits in Mark's realms. Asking for assistance, another vision occurred of someone who looked like a grandfather or great-grandfather. We perceived his name was Nelson. Asking what his story was, we perceived that he was a native American. He was tied to the land because he had made an oath to the land to steward it.

Again, we requested fog dispeller from the Father for the angels and then commissioned the angels for its use concerning Nelson the LHS. We asked angels to bring Nelson close.

Asked if creek bed was on Mark's dad's land, we discovered there was. Two small creeks flowed through Mark's father's land. We identified which of the two creeks were involved as this native American found

Mark from this creek bed, but he is tethered to the land through a vow he made to the land. I feel like the reason I can even see him is because Mark was living close to the area of the creek.

Having dealt with similar situations where a native American was tied to the land, let me describe a procedure I use to speak to them. In situations like this one, we commend the LHS for their willingness to steward the land, but discuss with them turning that stewardship over to the Lord, the Creator of the land itself, and let Him assign angels or whomever to steward the land. This LHS had taken it upon himself as his personal duty to steward the land and that is why he is remaining.

As I discussed the procedure, we could sense the great interest the LHS had in what I was saying, so speaking to him we commended Nelson for his stewardship of the land and his willingness to remain over the land, watching it. We suggested to him that the Lord of Hosts the Creator the land, He can steward it, and he could continue his destiny in the realms of Heaven because his destiny was not over. We proposed that he pass from this earth, for his destiny was not to remain in Mark's realms. He needed to step over into the realms of Heaven and when he stood before the Father, the Great Spirit, to call upon Him and ask for mercy. We asked if he would be willing to trust the Father, the Great Spirit, that He will bring another to steward the land from those living on the earth?

Nelson's question was could he relinquish his stewardship? When we told him, yes, he could, he immediately did so. We thanked him and told him, now he was going to receive his reward and his peace and rest.

He acknowledged that he was ready and explained that angels were going to come and get him. We then opened the silver channel and asked angels to take Nelson by the hand to lead him through the silver channel to his eternal rest. After his exit, we closed the silver channel.

We thanked the Father for Nelson's duty to the land, then requested the release of angels for the cleansing of the land and the creek bed due to the exit of this lingering human spirit.

We offered this testimony for the courts:

In the Court of Records, we would like to submit testimony that we have witnessed the exit of a lingering human spirit who was tied to the land as a steward. We are requesting the new steward in the Father's plan, who is living their life to be blessed with the stewardship of the land and to be given a relationship to the land in the wholeness and fullness of the plan of God, in Jesus' name.

We ask that what has been locked up, this land that has be locked up, would now be unlocked in Jesus' name.

We request the alignment, cleansing, purification, righteousness, and time sequencing of the land to be put back in order and alignment in the name of Jesus.

We had to end our engagement at that point but would continue it a short time later.

———— · ————

Chapter 5

Blended Lingering Spirits

I had been discussing with my seer how it was difficult to discern the name of the LHS we called Marjorie in an earlier session. We determined to do some digging to see what we could find out. It seemed as if it was a layered situation.

The question was, "Did we remove all of the LHS's?" We decided to look at the Guest Registry in spreadsheet form again sorting alphabetically by name.

> *Father, I ask for access to the Courts of Heaven through Jesus' realm, through His name. Jesus. I would like access to the Court of Records in the Guest Registry Office.*

We asked to look at our client, Mark's Guest Registry? We asked to sort the Guest Registry list alphabetically by First Name. A listing appeared and the first name was Angeline and then a Sylvia. Wanting to know more we found we could sort by Relationship to Mark. To dig even deeper we asked to search by Bloodline relatives.

After that sort was when we saw the name Marjorie (mentioned in the last chapter). Asking why we didn't I see it on the other sorts, he replied, "It is because she has exited. She has exit papers. We asked for the date of the exit and saw the date, June 9th which was the date we helped her transition. We asked if this person was a grandmother, great-grandmother, or an aunt? We were astonished at the reply.

We were told by the attendant that it was the blend where multiple spirits came together in the spirit. Two lingering human spirits in the waterless place, joined together for protection and companionship. Due to the relationship of one of the LHS's to Mark, they chose to go to Mark's realm. They made an agreement as human spirits to blend.

We did not have any information on how that worked, and the attendant was not volunteering any. However, we had the visual of the way we place a sheet of onion paper over another sheet of paper, and we can see through the onion paper and someone looking on would not see the two sheets of paper, but it would appear as one sheet of paper.

We were told that the two LHS's were watching out for each other in those places. *Essentially, they combined forces to jointly find a host.* The one that Marjorie was blended with is Sylvia who is a relation of Mark. She was not in the bloodline but was accepted into the bloodline, like being loosely related as an aunt. She may have been someone's girlfriend.

The name Marjorie was a nickname. Her name was Margaret, but she preferred Marjorie and her spirit man took that name even though the given name was Margaret. She liked Marjorie so they called her that.

With that information we understood that Sylvia was still present and was still in the lower spine. Even though they were blended, when Marjorie went, Sylvia stayed. They disengaged.

Father, in the name of Jesus, I speak to Sylvia in Mark's realms. Sylvia, come on out.

I ask the assistance of my angels and the angels assigned to me to help me minister to this lingering human spirit. Sylvia.

I speak to you very directly. You are not living in the area best suited for you. You are trespassing, and you cannot stay here. This isn't good for you, and it's not good for Mark.

Sylvia replied, "Well, it's been okay for me."

We replied, "Yes, but we have a little issue. Sylvia, have we just been hanging out here because we did not know where to go because Marjorie said it was good?"

"Yes," she replied.

"Well," we told her, "we know Marjorie went on in through the silver channel to her eternal destiny to a place where she could do business with the Creator, the Father who made you and loves you. He wants to do business with you."

We could detect that Sylvia wanted to do business with the Father, but she had some questions.

We replied to her, "You have some questions, and I am sure He can answer them. It would be better for you to ask Him your questions. Tell me why you have been afraid? Why have you been uncertain?"

Sylvia replied, "I did not know if He was trustworthy." She also had seen the angels but was not sure they were good.

We explained what happened when she passed away, "Angels came that day to get you when your body was at an end. Now, we have an opportunity to open the silver channel for you to go through. It will look like a tunnel. It will have light, and it will end in the third heaven where you can do business with the Father. You can ask Him for mercy. You can ask Jesus to speak for you."

Sylvia replied that she was tempted by the offer, and we replied, "Well, I appreciate that you're tempted to go, but guess what? We are not going to be able to give you a choice today. This is your graduation day. You will like it. I am sorry you did not know that the Father really loves you. He is crazy about you, and you get to have relationship with Him where you are headed. All you must do is ask for His mercy and say 'Father, have mercy on me,' and He will have mercy on you. He is not interested in filling up hell with people. He wants to fill up Heaven."

Father, thank you for this opportunity. I open the silver channel in the name of Jesus.

I ask for angels to come and escort Sylvia through the silver channel. Now, goodbye Sylvia. In the name of Jesus, I close the silver channel, Father.

I ask for more ministering angels to come to Mark's realms, to clean up all spiritual debris left by Sylvia, by her engagement with Marjorie and the debris left by Marjorie.

I ask for all things to come back into alignment.

I ask for the work of angels to bring all things into alignment, including the body realm, soul realm, and spirit realm.

I ask for all additional things left behind by the lingering human spirits Sylvia and Marjorie, that those things would be removed. If they are corrupt, they need to be destroyed, and I ask angels to destroy those things, Father.

I asked for the amendment of 'As if it Never Were' for Mark, and I ask for the amendment called the 'Sword of the Spirit' that the sword would excise anything additional that has been added to the DNA, the RNA, or the epigenome, that it would be spliced back.

I ask that any leakage of the DNA would be cauterized by the Sword of the Spirit now, in the name of Jesus.

With that Sylvia made her transition with the help of angels. We closed the silver channel to the rejoicing of Heaven.

———·———

Chapter 6

Gathering Tares

Continuing to learn from the engagement with Heaven, we prayed,

I ask for angels, Father, to go and retrieve seeds that are tares in Mark's spheres, sown by human spirits that were not his spirit.

I release harvesting angels to go and separate the wheat from the tares, because lingering human spirits have sown seeds in the realms of Mark's spirit.

I release harvesting angels to harvest wheat—the good harvest of their seed of the lingering human spirits and put them in the warehouse.

I ask for the tares to be separated out by these harvesting angels and for the tares to be destroyed in the fire of God.

I ask this for Mark's realms and area of any realm that the lingering human spirits sowed into or where they were lodged.

I ask for angels to do this now in the name of Jesus.

I ask for these things both in time and out of time, in Jesus' name.

It's a work inside a realm by angels and that a realm once cleansed of an unwanted guest, then this releases a harvest of what was sown in that realm. But since they were human spirits, they may have sown tares—not good seed. They may have sown a mixture. That is how this started. They sowed a mixture.

We had asked for the tares to be burned, and for the good seed sown to be harvested and stored in the warehouses although we did not know specifically what warehouses the good seeds were to go to.

We discovered that if it is good seed, it has multiplied because good seed multiplies. Some would go to Marjorie's warehouse, some would go to Sylvia's, and some would go to the warehouse of the host—Mark. They sowed seed but did not sow it in their field, but in Mark's, so he gets what amounts to a bonus—a recompense, because it was his field.

We can ask for reclamation in the court of reclamations and yes, we can do it retroactively. All things are possible.

Father, we ask permission to enter the Court of Reclamations. We are here with a request for the court.

We would like to enter a court case to reclaim seed that was good seed sown by previous lingering human spirits in Mark's realms.

We were then asked by someone in the court if we had authorization for that and we replied that we did. We continued...

Father, we request in the Court of Reclamations, in the name of Jesus, that all good seed sown by lingering human spirits in Mark's realms would be stored in the store houses according to Your perfect judgment and that all tares previously sown in his realms by lingering human spirits would be collected from Mark's realms and burned with fire.

This is a type of the cleansing of spiritual debris. We have been asking for the spiritual debris to be cleaned up once an LHS has been cleared. We also began asking for the seed that those lingering human spirits sowed as lingering human spirits in a host, that they be divided, and the tares taken be away and burned and that the good seed be stored in warehouses.

Lingering human spirits aware of the host and are usually aware when they are sowing seed. Some are aware that they are sowing seed. We must think of seed like a sound frequency.

> *A demonic guard will make a lingering human spirit sow sound frequencies into the hosts realms.*

These would be like the tares. They would be the bad seed or the seed that crowds out the good seed and results in what we would call physical harm to the body. Tinnitus, for example, could be one.

To clarify what she was hearing, we asked,

> *We are asking for the harvest of the seed that the lingering human spirit sowed, and we don't want the tares.*

If a demonic guard caused the LHS to release sound frequencies which cause torment, if there is a demonic guard sent to torment, the human spirit feels the torment and releases negative seed, which becomes tares, which becomes spiritual debris. The lingering human spirit who finds a host they have come to hide in or reside in, and they do not have a demonic guard, they may, being a spirit, see things that they sow in agreement with the host.

> *If they sow good things, they do so because they want their vessel that they are hiding in to remain in good shape.*

They agree with the good things that they have a discernment of because they have a sort of discernment that helps them agree for the good things.

This is not a principle of the Father. **He created one body for one spirit**; and interlopers and intruder spirits, lingering human spirits—whatever we are going to call them—these human spirits have found a host, but they are operating against the principles and laws of a holy God. The only exception would be of a pregnant mother carrying children and those spirit(s) are still hosted within her temporarily. That is how it was created to be. That is how Yahweh created it. A pregnant woman is really the only exception to the one spirit—one body rule. The spirit of a man in a man is divine.

The spirit of a man or the spirit of a human is divinely matched to their soul and to their body.

It is a divine creative act by the will of Yahweh, so for a lingering human spirit to find a host and move in creates a corruption. Even though they can sow good seed, they are doing it from their vested interests that their hosts remain in good condition.

The demons will find the LHS because the demon is drawn to things. A demon will find them, put them under assignment, and torment them to release negativity and negative sound vibrations into the host, and it is worse for the host thereafter—far worse.

We have Satan who sends a demon, who finds a human spirit. He knows that arrangement is corrupt and *because of the corruption,* he has a legal right to then torment the human spirit, who then is forced to torment their host against their will. Then, the LHS cannot find a way home or find a way out. They are locked in between a rock and a dry place.

> *The work of redemption includes the work of opening the silver channel and offering exit to a human spirit to a truer relationship with the Father and the Creator.*

Human spirits tremble in fear at demonic guards. The trembling is a frequency within the host causing havoc in body parts, soul realms, and even spiritual senses. For instance, the pathway of dreaming in the night. They are responsible for scary dreams. In the night seasons, the host receives a scary dream because of the trembling of the human spirit in the realm who is being tormented by a demon. Remember, demons are lazy, but they are just smart enough to be able to figure out that they can torment a human spirit, enslaving it to itself and forcing it to create havoc in the host of the living.

Our attendant, who had been so helpful was named Gerald. We wanted to return for more revelation in a future time, but he reminded us that it was good for us to take this slow. We agreed.

———·———

Chapter 7

The Guest Registry

Engaging Heaven again for further instruction on lingering human spirits (LHS's), we discussed what Gerald, the attendant in the Registry Office had taught us about wheat and tares and about blended spirits. We also were taught about the spreadsheet (aka Unwanted Guest Registry) and the ways we could sort the data, but they also hinted at something on the spreadsheet. They mentioned that we could determine what type of entities were on that Unwanted Guest Registry spreadsheet. Apparently, the Guest Registry (the spreadsheet) contained information about more than just lingering human spirits. We wanted to know what other entities were listed on that spreadsheet. We discovered several. This is not an exhaustive list because we are just beginning to discover them.

One of the first entities we discovered was an imp. Imps are pestering little evil creatures who incessantly annoy their host or others.

> *Imps are low-level creatures sent to annoy and aggravate us. Imps have no good intention.*

Without wanting to investigate dark places to find out more, it is a low-level demon and one of the characteristics of it is it is *highly mobile*. It springs and hops from one thing to another. Just when we think we see it, it has hopped over to something else. It does that ping pong thing where we can hardly catch it or nail it down. That is what it feels like. I saw that (or had the impression of it) when I was looking in the registry.

We wanted to know what other things were in the registry. We were instructed to go to a classroom on the sixth floor where Gerald would tutor us.

When we arrived, Gerald was waiting on us. We began, "We've returned to pick up where we left off about what we can share with us regarding lingering human spirits and the Guest Registry. We are willing to learn, and we are asking you to be our teacher. We are willing to be students. We are willing to be students of creation and have ears that hear and eyes that see."

We began to see a color that looked like the reflection of a flame. It does not have a color. It is bright white. I am not looking directly at a bright white flame, but I am near a bright white flame, and I can see the reflection of it in the space I am in. It is purifying. We paused a moment to receive the torch and understood that it was connected to the revelation about lingering human spirits and that we were going to receive more information about receiving new knowledge. This torch had a purifying effect that we could engage with.

We were given what appeared like welder's goggles and began seeing into an ancient forge with evil creatures working to heat mettle. They appeared as hybrid creatures. They had some human features, but not entirely. It was not a happy place, rather it was a place of torment. Gerald explained that it was essentially what Noah saw in his day. It was a place full of licentiousness and full of horror with an awful atmosphere. These creatures were making chains and shackles.

We were told to look and describe what happened next. A brilliant white light like a starburst opened in the realm where these creatures were doing this. The creatures ran for cover. They were absolutely petrified of this powerful being that this white flame star explosion represents. It began moving around the room where they were, and was picking up things. They were picking up what looked like pieces of DNA—pieces of a human. Continuing to look we could see body parts that the angel was gathering. What he was doing did not even seem hard for this being. He appeared to have interrupted what had been taking place.

When we release the Angels of the Host to retrieve soul parts and those parts that have been traded on illegally by dimensional beings, we are plundering. We were witnessing a plunder of Satan's realm and a retrieval of missing parts. The angelic being was on a retrieval mission. As we continued to look at the white star explosion, we could see the being inside it who had a human-like form.

This angelic being was more armor-clad than we typically had seen, but the armor was not armor like we think of armor. The armor was the light, and he was made of it. It is not on him. He is made of it. The angel looked at us and nodded.

We were witnessing a retrieval of human souls and spirit parts. We were looking at the retrieval of a part of a human spirit that had been fragmented and parts of a human soul that had been fragmented. We were looking at the retrieval of both from a pit of hell. This information can be found in the Registry.

We came to learn that whenever this angel showed up, whatever he is there for retrieval of, he does not reach out for it, but it is magnetized to him, but just the things that he is there to collect and retrieve. Those things are attracted to his being. We could not see where they were coming from, but they were coming into his being. It is like he was a big magnet and everything he was there to get—he was getting.

This is what occurs when we send angels on retrieval for soul parts and fragmented spirits, even fragmented body parts including retrieval of DNA parts. All three realms can be fragmented."[8]

Maximize the retrieval of fragmented parts is a work of redemption. It is plundering the enemy's camp. It is taking back what is rightfully belonging to others that have been stolen, or traded on, or traded away.

Some of these parts have been traded by people intentionally, not knowing they were making a trade with evil. Some have been stolen by demons on assignment. Some of these parts and pieces have come because of ancient trades in the bloodline and some still today are intentionally trading with evil on these things through ritual sacrifice and the propagation of humanity for sacrifice. Some have been lab created for darkness. Some parts have simply been lost due to terror, trauma, moments of terror and trauma, and the overwhelming effects of great fear. Some have been harvested in moments of medical anesthesia. Some have intentionally come from the use of addictive substances, and some would be humans who have been stolen from as these parts were stolen from them in the depth and mire of chemical depression—depression that is unintentional like by a drug or by the corruption that is on the bloodline.

---

[8] The three realms being the soul realm, the spirit realm, and the body realm, with the DNA being part of the body realm and therefore can be fragmented.

As we were receiving this information, another angel appeared with a message for us:

Woe to those who fight.

Woe, woe, woe to those who fall in ignorance, for the Lord God Almighty did not create children of His to walk in ignorance.

Woe to those who have not understood you cannot serve both masters; you cannot serve two kingdoms. You cannot serve dark and light. You cannot live on the boundary line between the two.

As the angel spoke, we could see the boundary line between the two. It is a horrible, spatial place. It is neither wicked, nor love and light—it is zombie-like. It is like watching a human who has become a zombie. It is less emotive, just vacant, absent, void. It is a chaos of void.

The Court Case

Wanting to know how to utilize this information, Gerald began to show a court case. He showed a repentance for the ignorance of spiritual things explaining that the goal of the verdict in this court case is the paperwork for the Angels of the White Flame[9] to

---

[9] The name of the angel mentioned earlier in this chapter.

retrieve splintered, fragmented, spiritual beings—spirit parts, soul parts, and body parts or DNA parts.

From the Courts of Heaven, receive a ruling—a verdict from the righteous judge, as He sits to hear those who will:

- Repent for the ignorance of the ages,
- Repent for the work of the religious spirit,
- Repent for the embracing religion that shuts down the power of God and that negates and nullifies the holy work of the Spirit of the Lord.

The hope of Satan is that humanity would walk in lack of discernment of spiritual things, that they would so forget who they are, that they're never able to shake off the slumber that has fallen on their spirit, so he may plunder the spirit realm, so he may plunder spirit fragments.

Why Do They Linger?

We have wondered why a human spirit would choose to linger in a realm of uncertainty, because we have been thinking from the knowledge of the Tree of Life. But to the human spirit, who has never eaten of the fruit of the Tree of Life from their spirit man, they do not have this nutrition—which translates to their discernment of the realm of spirit. When they have been released from their body because they have never practiced their spirit, their spirit slumbers—it sleeps deeply. The jarring that comes as the human spirits exit from physical flesh in the path of transition to eternal rest, that spirit never has partaken of this, and it operates in ignorance is tremendously sad. It is *not* the plan of God!

These human spirits are at risk to be captured by demonic entities. But sometimes they place their parts that are split, fragmented, or splintered in a place for ungodly sale and trade to other realms, to other timelines, and other dimensional, or celestial beings. These are some wild things.

Murder Victims

Let me give an example of a murder victim. We had to pause momentarily and ask her angels to come near to help her spirit minister to her soul while she gained this information. We may need to pause and do the same.

When someone is murdered whose spirit had never been awakened to the spiritual dynamics that the spirit is capable of (because the human is made in the likeness of God), the human spirit has a level of spiritual understanding, but that spirit is meant to be watered, matured, loved, and blessed. Just like we would do to the body, and to the soul, we would curate the image of the likeness of God in us and nurture it. Having received that, then the enemy comes to remove that part of a person. How would we remove the spirit from the body? We would murder the body. We kill the body.

The result is we have a soul part and spirit part, which we separate forever. The anguish of that is indescribable to the person. Then we splinter both and we put them up for sale.

Now, we have a commodity and we put them up for sale in trans-dimensional realms that occupy time pockets, time realms, time spaces, time folds, and time transitions. These are now what we are trading on. This is enabled trade. Do we see now why the Father would have such penalty for murder, if the result of murder is so heinous, so opposite to the plan of God? Wickedness trades on these things.

If we are involved in the work of redemption, we must understand how valuable the human spirit is. A captured human spirit is an asset to the kingdom of darkness. Not only are they capturing human spirits to enslave them to torment humanity; they are using the fragmented pieces to *develop races* and *make trades*.

There is something about a human spirit fragment that other-dimensional beings have knowledge of. The essence of it is it is a thing that can only be created by the Creator so, it is highly valued. The enemy does not value it properly though. They do not value it to esteem it. They value it *for what they can use it for*, and the soul part is similar—that is why some experience the fragmenting of the soul.

We can fragment the soul of a person and not kill them, but with the loss of the spirit comes death. When we are rescuing a human spirit from a realm and we have discovered it, for instance in another human, and it is under torment by a demon guard—*the thing we want to do is also redeem the spirit part because we may not be looking at the entire human spirit.* Chances are, *we are looking at a partial human spirit.* We can know the difference by looking in the registry at will.

Here is some great news! There are things here in the realms of Heaven that even Satan does not know. *We* have the knowledge of Heaven, which is hidden from the demonic, but they are after this knowledge.

The Antidote

The antidote for this is for the human to walk in the light, walk in the secrets of the Kingdom of God, and walk in righteousness, having received Jesus as Savior.

So many things were in the life of Jesus that caused his human spirit and soul to be so untouchable by this darkness—by this demonic trade. Even simple things like rest and enjoyment and fellowship, and what Paul said, 'Think on these things...the things that are true.'[10] All of that (referring to Philippians 4:8) is so helpful for the human spirit to have a buffer and have an inherent likeness to God that the spirit and soul of that person become untouchable by darkness. The Scripture tells us how light, and darkness cannot mix.[11]

---

[10] Philippians 4:8

[11] 2 Corinthians 6:14

> *The principle is that*
> *the more we are in the light,*
> *the more we are untouchable*
> *to these things.*

Yet, that is where that is where the danger is—*when we are not in the light we are at real risk.* Remember the boundary line that appeared as a dimensional space of the zombie land (as we called it) where we are neither hot, nor cold—we are just vague—we can be pushed either way. We have no rock; we have never determined to stand or not stand. We are just blown in the wind, and it is the worst place. It is the worst time.

———·———

Chapter 8

Spirit Fragmentation

Mark (our client) volunteered to be a guinea pig for understanding more of this, so we accessed the Court of Records and entered the Guest Registry Office asking to see Mark's Guest Registry. We asked to sort by 'Type of Fragmentation,' and they asked which type of fragmentation: spirit or soul. We were seeking information concerning spirit fragmentation at that time.

Under the column of Trades was the listing of a spirit fragmentation. We learned we could sort within a previous sort and drill down to the information that we were needing to see.

As we saw the words on the spreadsheet, the words became visual, and we could see the story as opposed to reading the record. In this case one could see a teenager and a young boy about seven.

We were looking at traumas that caused fragmented spirit pieces and spirit fragments. They were on the Mark's timeline. We were looking at a timeline. We were seeing that the trades were from moments of shock, trauma, fear, projection of trauma, projection of fear, or projection of shock.

An assistant in the Guest Registry Office came to assist us as we wanted more understanding about what we were seeing. He explained that Heaven has a record of spirit fragmentation, and it has timeframes. In the case of this client, we chose to simply read it as the visual images from Mark's timeline that we could discern.

We saw a boy who was about seven. We also saw a teenager who was about thirteen. The teenager was around water. We also saw a 17-year-old. We had no further clues about the 17-year-old visually, but the attendant explained that the spirit fragments were stolen or taken. In an opportune moment, the enemy took a part of Mark's human spirit. We were present to redeem that back.

The assistant reiterated that we would know all these details had happened unless we came to look.

Now, to deal with this matter we were going to need a court room scenario which is the simplest way. We stepped into the Mercy Court on behalf of the young Mark and the 13-year-old Mark saying, "I first repent for ignorance. I also repent for lacking spiritual discernment. I repent for not working with one's angels, and I repent for falling in line with fear."

Proceeding to the 17-year-old, the repentance was different. The attendant explained, "This is a repentance for how the soul realm leads us, by something that we know is wrong. The soul will get scared because something is off limits and it knows it, but it is going to go touch that thing anyway. It is the essence of sin which is *rebellion* and *idolatry*. Those are things we could repent for regarding the 17-year-old. There is something the spirit experiences as an excitement that is just a wicked introduction of sin to the person."

Resonance of the Spirit

The attendant then showed how the spirit has a resonance. If our soul led our spirit and begin to resonate with dark instead of light, then the spirit receives a disharmony from its creation. At the same time, it can be translated as 'since it doesn't know.' It is just not how the spirit was created by the Spirit of God who is light; but the soul translates the experience as an excitement. Nevertheless, it is a resonance, and it must make it the resonance, all the *while our soul is off doing its thing. At that moment,* the enemy snatches a portion of our spirit.

It is a horrible thing, because it is like we are agreeing with a trade or maybe we are agreeing with Satan and Satan goes, 'Ha ha! I've got you!' We do not even know we have been gotten. We do not even know we lost something, or we left some piece of us behind.

Father, we request access to Mercy Court this day.

I repent for ignorance, for lack of spiritual discernment.

I repent for not working with my angels. I repent for falling in line with fear. I repent for rebellion and for allowing my soul to lead me into sin, in Jesus' name.

The Key

We have been given a key—as a ministry for the unlocking of angelic host to go on search and retrieval missions. Specifically, Gerald said, "This key is from Jesus since He owns all pieces in all realms. We can go to the Court of Angels to release this key to the angelic hosts that *they may go on a retrieval errand to unlock any gateway, path, or gate that has been shut* against the retrieval of the spiritual fragments.

- This key unlocks doors, gates, realms, wormholes, fabric folds, and time fabric folds.
- It unlocks access points of spiritual dimensions and gives the angelic hosts permission.
- It gives an entrance to retrieve from every place that the spirit part has been subsequently traded, hidden, enslaved, or unjustly captured and put on a shelf or stored in a warehouse for future use.

An angel appeared who had come to get the key. On the back of his wing was the word 'Plunder.' Giving him the key, we commissioned him to plunder and retrieve all missing parts and bring them back to where they were supposed to be. We then began to see very luscious fruit and a honeycomb. We were looking at the sweetness of a human spirit in wholeness.

Wondering if we needed to do some specific things to bring the person to freedom we were answered via a vision where we saw a calendar and began to pray into what was being seen.

> *We ask for the establishment of timeline correction and seasons in Mark's realms.*
>
> *We ask for the spirit parts of Mark that have been retrieved by the angel who has plundered due to the repentance in Your courts today—we are requesting that the spirit fragments be re-introduced to <u>all appropriate timelines and seasons in Mark's realms and in his book</u>.*
>
> *We are asking for <u>a mending, a splicing, a reinsertion of the spirit fragments to the spirit of Mark</u>.*
>
> *We celebrate their return. I agree with Heaven that this is sweet—like honey and desirable as fruit.*

It made us wonder about something Eve said, in the Garden of Eden. We wondered if, in the deception, she could not see the desirability of maintaining her spirit in wholeness. "Was her spirit fragmented at that point and at that point in time?" We wondered.

Satan's goal was to be able to introduce a new frequency and that vibration of the spirit. Eve's soul overrode her spirit, so it gave a portion of it to another. I think her soul gave in to the influence of the evil and was given to another frequency.

Timeline Corrections

As I have worked with Heaven in the Courts and classrooms, I have learned about different impacts to what we would refer to as our timeline. When we have experienced interferences in our timeline due to fragmentation, we may be left with the feeling that we are *out of sync* in some area of our lives. At that point we need to request a mending of any folds or breaches in our timeline and that they be reset to the design of the Father. This will result in a sense of wholeness and completeness in the individual receiving this type of ministry. This can be accomplished in the Court of Times and Seasons.

Our engagement with Gerald was over at this point, but we continued to learn from him a few days later.

Chapter 9

Soul Fragmentation

A visit to the Court of Records Guest Registry Office was for this day as we sought to view Mark's registry. We were looking for fragmentation.

First however, we decided to look at the listing of spirit fragments to see if there were any nuances to what was in there before. We asked to sort by spirit fragments. Looking at what we had worked on previously with Mark, we could see the input, 'Fragments Reconciled.' If a matter has been taken care of, it will say that it is Reconciled. The attendant pointed out, "It's what you search for."

It is what we are looking for that we can see. If we are not looking for it, we may not see it.

That explains why we have not seen all that needed to be seen when ministering to a person because we had not asked to see it. The verse, "you have not because you ask not,"[12] came to mind. We must appear in the Office of the Registry and really ask for it. It is still the principle of "The more specific the request, the more specific the answer we will receive."

That is why we want to be specific as to what we are looking for, which is why I want to know what else is on that account. What kind of things are included in that list?

For instance, now I would like to search for soul fragmentation for Mark. We will find the information in the Guest Register of the person because the register has data on a lot more than just LHS's. It includes all sorts of "guests" that one may have picked up along the way.

When I was first introduced to the Guest Registry was a couple of years ago. I was shown the Guest Registry and called it that because it reminded me of the Guest Registry we might sign at a hotel or funeral home. I was originally referring to evil spirits or demons, not merely LHS's on assignment but now I know the registry can contain more than just LHS's, demons, or whatever.

I wanted to know what else we needed to be looking for because we have come across some strange stuff on occasion, and I do not want something to slide off the

---

[12] James 4:2

table because we were not looking for it or did not know to look for it. Heaven pointed out to us:

---
*If we know to look for it,
it cannot stay hidden.*

With that understanding, we continued and requested to sort the database for Soul Fragmentation.

Again, the words on the Guest Registry assumed a visual context and it felt like we were looking at an event timeline. We could see infanthood but this one was pre-toddler. In Mark's behalf we looked to see if any others were listed and found one related to an event in Mark's late twenties or early thirties and it was related to an employer relation.

The next thing on the event timeline was the scene of a jungle, so we asked Mark if he had been near a jungle environment at some point. He could not recall any, so we asked assistance from the Court of Records where we were. We discovered that the event occurred when Mark flew over one a jungle which he had done on four occasions in the last few years. We will discuss more about this in a few pages.

Infanthood Fragmentation

We went back to the infanthood fragmentation that had been discerned earlier. Looking at the registry for this, one could see that someone was severely disappointed. They had dashed hopes. It was from the maternal side. As more clarity came, we sensed that Mark's mother had been either tricked or deceived, or she had an expectation that was not met. The plot of the enemy was to bring harm between the mother and the infant. At that point in time, the infant had no guards up on their soul, but the infant's soul picked up on this extreme disappointment, so the fragmentation came.

Wondering what the repentance for that would be, the attendant replied, "As the infant had no sin in the matter, the pathway for repentance was the forgiveness of the mother for dashed expectations and holding expectations that were not given by God. Then, request the restoration of that soul part."

With that request we wanted to know where the soul part is and if the registry had that information. The answer came in an understanding. We know what it feels like when we put a jigsaw puzzle away and we leave one piece out of the box, it is still in the house, right? It is not lost, but it is not used. It is not where it should go. It is still around. It is just not connected. That is what it feels like. Fortunately, we could not see a trade on that soul fragment, nor did we see a captivity of that soul fragment. We did not see any fear around it and there were no demons around it. It has just happened, and it is like it is lying in Mark's realms needing to be connected.

We determined to go through with the process we were perceiving and watch what happened.

Father, we request access to the Mercy Court regarding this soul part from Mark's infanthood.

I forgive his mother for the soul realm expectations, for holding expectations not given by You.

I bless her, forgive her, and release her in Jesus' name.

I request restoration of that soul part now, in the name of Jesus.

Looking at the registry and next to that timed event, it said 'Mended.'

To retrieve the soul part, it seemed as if the angel had to go a long way to get it, although no distance really exists in that realm. It seemed as if an angel had been assigned to retrieve the soul part but was not the Angel of the White Flame we had seen in a prior engagement. It felt like an angel picking up a baby. It was not a large project for the angel but rather run-of-the-mill.

Sensing we may be done with this registry entry we asked, "Is there anything else we need to do on that one? Is this mended soul fragment restored to Mark's soul realm? Is there anything to do?"

We were instructed to thank the Father for restoration. The Father loves the whole soul. He made the soul, so He has pleasure at the redemption of lost parts.

We replied,

We honor this part. We honor the soul fragment that has been lost but now is found and mended to Mark's whole soul. We welcome you back. We embrace you. We have needed you, and we honor your position and want you to integrate with the whole soul. We thank You for this, Father, in Jesus' name.

It felt like that was a part of a tiny event line that has been mended. "Is there any cleansing for the soul part?" we asked.

The attendant replied, "A soul part receives the benefit of the whole, so if the whole soul is in a good state, then the integrated part receives the ministry of that."

"That is good to know," we replied.

The Church Situation

The next soul fragment had to do with a situation in Mark's thirties. We described what was being perceived. This is the one that felt like there was a person in authority over Mark, who was near him. That is why it feels like an employer. The fragmentation to the soul was some sort of a wound—which would be like the sense of where we are doing the best we can, the best we know how, the best we were able to do—and instead of the person honoring the best that we could offer, they dishonored all of it. It was like they measured Mark's soul, and he came up wanting.

Mark asked if this was an event that occurred with a church if we could not perceive that. We confirmed that it was and then Mark knew the situation in question.

We then asked, "What is the path of the restoration of the soul fragment? What is the path of forgiveness to the perpetrators of the pain of that original trauma or the original wound? Where is the soul fragment? Has it been traded?"

We perceived it had been traded by a religious spirit. It felt like the wicked entity scored on this trade, like somewhere a tally was kept that this trade happened and because the religious spirit obtained this soul fragment, he got extra points for it.

We wondered if the trauma moment was a plot of the enemy that was intentional for the trade of a soul fragment of Mark's soul. Think about coaches and teachers and parents and grandparents, where the person in that role and whatever season they are in, that even when someone is doing the best that they can, it can be met with total misunderstanding. I guess that is the mildest way to put that which often brings a fragmentation—how the enemy would set that up for an intentional soul fragment that he could then trade on. In Mark's case, the event was all about a religious spirit who was the perpetrator.

With a situation like this, there is more that we must do to get the soul part back. We must request nullifying of the trade on the grounds that it was immorally done. It was done in alignment with darkness or through deception of the religious spirit, like had the human known they were being used by a religious spirit they would have had another thought, but they were deceived or ignorant. It is ignorance. Remember the verse in Hosea (4:6) which says, "my people are destroyed for lack of knowledge."

We then requested access to the Mercy Court to deal with this situation on Mark's behalf.

> *I request access to the Mercy Court in relation to the soul fragment taken from Mark in his early thirties.*
>
> *Father, I choose forgiveness of those involved in the situation—the pastor, the elders, and the other people that were involved in the whole thing. I forgive them, bless them, and release them in Jesus' name.*
>
> *I request a nullifying of the trade of the soul part on the grounds that it was immorally done or done in alignment with darkness or through the deception of the religious spirit. I ask for a cancellation of the trade.*
>
> *I ask for the return of the soul part to its original design, and I request any impact to Mark's timelines be made it as if it were never damaged.*

Following that prayer, an angel with 'Plunder' written on his wings was present. He came into the courtroom to get the paperwork. It was not the very same angel as before, so we assumed this to be a rank of Plundering Angels.

We asked the attendant, "When this soul part is mended back to the whole, is there any ministry to the soul fragment?"

This soul fragment needs cleansing because it has been traded, and it has been touched by darkness. It needs ministry.

We ask for ministering angels to minister wholeness to this soul, bringing the soul part back online to the cleansing power of the mind of Christ Jesus.

We minister the mind of Christ to the soul part, its' righteousness, its' beloved status, and its' integration to the perfection of its design, in Jesus' name."

Looking again at the registry, beside that entry, it had the words, 'In Process' which makes sense, because Mark was an adult when the event happened, so that soul part coming back and being inserted and integrated in is so tangible.

Darkness wants that soul fragment, and they have need of it; and because they cannot create it, they steal it. When the soul fragment is fully integrated and cleansed, having been ministered to (probably when we are asleep—possibly in the next sleep cycle), it will come back online.

We could see the ministering angels waiting. These angels are beautiful. They are very passion-filled angels. They love the soul. They are very careful with the soul.

They are very nurturing, and they want the best. They represent complete love.

We receive that, and we ask for the ministry of the mind of Christ to the lost soul part.

We say to the soul part, you are esteemed. We welcome you back.

We have need of you to be whole, and we honor the part you play in the soul realm.

What Happened in the Jungle?

Having finished ministering to the church situation we proceeded to the next situation—the one involving the jungle. It felt wicked in every way. Mark did not know he was traversing over land that was defiled and had a right, due to some wicked agreement, that released soul hunters. These were in the spirit realm, and Mark gave legal agreement by trespassing on their land or their territory, even though he merely flew over it on the airliner. Someone was hunting souls for the purpose of trade. No religious spirit was involved. However, it was a defilement of the land. It was about the release of bounty hunters for the capture of human souls.

Profane worship and a ritual sacrifice were probably done on the land for the purpose of trading in the spirit realm by engaging bounty hunters that would capture the soul fragment of people so that it could use it in the purpose of their trade.

The path of redemption would be the appearing in the Court of Titles and Deeds for the annulment of the trade since Mark had no knowledge of the trespass. Those who had released the bounty hunters and what they had done was through wickedness and evil, and not according to the principles of the owner of the land, which is the Lord. Their defilement of the land had created a prison and that is where that is where the soul fragment was.

We asked the attendant about the status of the soul fragment and were told that it had been traded again and now there are claims of ownership. It had crossed over into ownership where the other two (soul fragments) had not. It was being contested as an ownership claim because of the trade involved. The demons were saying Mark crossed over their land and he had to pay the tax for crossing the land.

We challenged the demons as they had done this to Mark in total deception. They were totally trespassing on the Lord's land based on the resurrection of Jesus Christ. That defense quickly shut the demons up.

Then we saw someone who looked like a pirate. He was the one claiming ownership of the soul part and that we would need to resolve the ownership claim in the Court of Titles and Deeds.

We request access to the Court of Titles and Deeds, and we request the annulment of the trade of Mark's soul part as he had no knowledge of the trespass on the land, or of the bounty hunters, or of any of the subsequent trades.

We request cancellation of not only that trade but also the cancellation of all ownership claims that are not to You, the Lord of Hosts.

We request the retrieval and return of this soul part based on the blood of Jesus.

The prayer was based on the blood of Jesus because Mark was in covenant through the blood, therefore that is the superior covenant. We were invoking the covenant through the blood.

Thank you, Father for the verdict.

Thank you for so totally overwhelming the enemy that he has even relinquished his hold on Mark's soul part before the verdict.

At this point, we were instructed to request that the Angel of the White Flame rather than the Angel of Plunder be sent to retrieve the missing part. We then asked the ministering angels to minister healing, nurture, and everything they do to bring wholeness.

The ministering angels cleanse, purify, restore, oil, water, and bring back online according to the original blueprint of design—the soul fragment. If the soul fragment has memory, they cleanse, purify, and eliminate memories that are not the memories of the original design. Concerning the memories gained while it was in captivity, the ministering angels eliminate them like clipping out a filmstrip, so that it is restored to the person in fullness. It comes back to we like it has been to the mechanic shop. Everything has been put back where it needs to be.

Regarding whether any corrections or adjustments needed to the persons timeline we learned that anytime we sense time has been affected, simply ask for the "Amendment of As if it Never Were."

Father, in your court today, as an amendment to this case, we request the 'Amendment of As if it Never Were.'

We also request that the soul part be washed with water.

The best news is that soul fragments, once restored are very resilient. This co-laboring between saints and angels does not just put the person back into the right time, it completes the time, so the soul feels whole.

A Relationship to Dementia

What can be done regarding dementia? We were made to understand that trauma, memory, and brain function are related to dementia regarding chemical aspects of the brain. The enemy is wicked beyond imagination seeking to steal what he cannot create where he cannot manufacture. He can manufacture some things, but he cannot manufacture a soul or a spirit, so he hunts them down, steals them, and fragments them with traumatic experiences. He will take it from a lingering human spirit, or he will take it from a human spirit in a vessel. He seeks the soul to destroy and operates against both soul and spirit equal in value to his greedy lack and effect for trade.

> *Remember that God is a jealous God. He is not willing to give up any piece of soul, any piece of spirit, or any piece of DNA that he has created after His image and in His likeness.*

His desire is for the full and complete integration of the whole and that the intent and purpose of the mission of Jesus Christ was for the legalities to be in place for His rescue, retrieval, and re-creation of each of His children.

This is what Jesus was so upset with the Pharisees and the Sadducees for—they withheld this information from the population. They knew the trades that were taking place which is simply evil.

One falls into deception like that through pride and through agreement with the enemy that they would put their throne above God's throne.

We wanted to check to see if things were complete concerning the jungle situation. We asked the attendant and beside the registry listing for that fragmentation, we saw 'In Process' and 'Progressing.'

Inquiring if any other soul fragments were in the registry, we discovered one more related to his middle daughter who had married first. It was around the time of her divorce and felt like a soul with disappointment, dashed hopes, dashed expectations, fortunately this one is not one was not traded on. It was simply floating around in Mark's realm. Satan had not found it yet. He does not have an innumerable number of demons which is why he uses LHS's. That number is growing, but the number of demons is not.

Pathway for Restoration

The pathway for restoration on this fragmentation was simply forgiveness of self and grace toward all. We informed mark that this could be some sort of accusation against him.

We request access to the Mercy Court on behalf of the soul fragment that was taken from Mark around the time of his daughter's divorce. Mark chooses, in this court to forgive himself.

We paused to ascertain the accusations that were outstanding against Mark in this situation. We identified that one accusation is that Mark lacked some type of contribution to her life or her ex-husband's life, and that the divorce was the result. It was an accusation linking him to the broken relationship.

Mark began,

Regarding the accusation. I agree with the adversary quickly. I confess it as sin. I repent, and I ask that the blood of Jesus to cover that accusation that I lacked some contribution to their lives that resulted in their divorce. I ask for your blood to cover that.

I request the return and retrieval of the soul part through the blood of Jesus.

We ask for the ministering angels to receive the soul part, make it whole, cleanse it, bring it back to the perfection of its original design.

I welcome this soul fragment. I honor you and we want you to know that you are needed. I bless you to be integrated into the whole. It was not the Father's plan for you to have been separated from the whole of the soul, but by His goodness, you have been restored and this is a point of joy.

Father, I also request the Amendment of 'As if it Never Were' related to the soul fragment that had been removed from me.

Looking again at the registry it said about the soul fragment, "Mending," but it did not say "Mended."

Father, we just praise Your name that You are interested in the whole, and You are interested in eradication of any corruption or lack due to corruption. Thank You for that.

We did one final check on the Guest Registry and saw no more entries, but we had learned quite a lot in this series of engagements. However, we had some more learning to do.

———·———

Chapter 10

Body Fragmentation

The one other area we had not covered concerned DNA fragments. We had done the spirit realm, and the soul realm, and now the body realm.

Turning to the attendant we said, "We would like to see the sorting of DNA fragments. Are there any DNA fragments?"

Again, the way we saw what was in the Guest Registry in the form of a vision. To view this information (at least this time) required the use of Fog Dispeller. We requested Fog Dispeller of the Father and then commissioned the angels to the full use of it as we were seeking this information.

Because we were dealing with DNA, which are building blocks of amino acids, we had to look at it differently. With certain conditions a person is missing chromosomes which are long DNA molecules, while in others they have too many chromosomes. Our search needed to be refined.

We had seen an image of a project made of Legos; the children's toy made up of plastic blocks. In the image one could we see where Legos were missing. We were instructed to sort by Lack of Additional Building Blocks.

DNA is also a blueprint. It tells the amino acid where to express. Some genetic conditions result when a strand is missing, while others occur when we have too many strands. We can search whether it is missing or added. In either case it results in a corruption. Then we would also have the option of a corruption of one of the intact DNA that has been affected. If there are too many or too little of the right number, but one of the right numbers has been affected, like with Down's Syndrome, there is an additional component. We also have corruption because of environmental things, medical procedures, pharmakeia, etc.

We requested to see a holographic image of a representation of Mark. We asked to see a body scan to reveal any missing DNA. We did not see anything but heard the word, musculoskeletal. We were looking geographically on the body.

I asked, if this was related to the feet and legs and we could see on the scan the right ankle being highlighted. We did not know why.

We asked if this was a piece of DNA that was missing, but it was not. It was a piece of DNA that was corrupted.

The next piece of information we needed to know regarding this was how did this come about? It was a result of bloodline ancestry we were told.

The pathway for restoration for replacement of the corrupted DNA in this situation was explained to us.

Procedure for the Return of Perfected DNA

We were instructed to go to the healing hospital and request the "Procedure for Return of Perfected DNA."

Following those instructions, we accessed the healing hospital With that information we continued our journey and checked Mark into the healing hospital for the Procedure for the Return of Perfected DNA."

We paused to repent on Mark's behalf for the sins of his bloodline ancestry.

I want to go on record. I repent for the sins of blood line ancestry that caused this corruption of the DNA to be passed to Mark. Father, I forgive them. I bless them and release them.

I ask that this corruption would be stopped passing further and that the perfected DNA would be restored to Mark's body in Jesus' name.

I ask for the substance of the DNA to be returned to the substance of the body in the name of Jesus. I ask for complete restoration of all DNA strands and code regarding feet and legs, movement of the musculoskeletal range and proteins for the muscle. I ask for this in Jesus' name, in the Healing Hospital at the hands of angels for Mark.

Since the DNA was not missing, merely corrupted, angels did not have to be sent to retrieve anything. In a brief discussion following this we realized we did not have to know what the specific iniquity was that was responsible for the corruption.

The angel assisting us said, "Think of the body like land. Did the sin on the land or the sin of the body which equated to a corruption of some DNA? It could be so for any illness, any malady, anything that is not perfection."

We recalled a situation where we ministered along those same lines to a young man with Asperger's Syndrome? It was DNA that got messed with. We were assured that we had been on the right track in the ministry to him.

These were things that we were learning, and patterns that would assist us in the precision of it and for the ministry of it.

We had been asking for the pathway for wholeness in these areas and we realized Heaven had a lot more to show us concerning DNA and restoration in that arena—essentially a whole university of information.

We have learned that the enemy can steal or corrupt spirit, soul, and body, and we wanted to know how to bring freedom. We want to be pressing in for this because there is so much more to learn.

We knew what we were learning would circle back to the subject of LHS's somehow since that is what got us started. Knowing we have more to learn about the Guest Registry and how it will help us understand how to even deal with the intrusion of celestial beings or underwater beings since we have dealt with those on occasion. We now know that we can look at that list and find out who the boss is. That is helpful to know.

It is easier to gain the knowledge of these things from heavenly realms rather than try to do it in the earth realm under the second Heaven, which wants to provide some corruption of what we are looking at (what the Apostle Paul described as seeing through a glass darkly). It feels like we are looking through a glass darkly. But when we have stepped into the realms of Heaven to see what angels are showing us or what registries we can see, it is clearer. Occasionally the use of Fog Dispeller will be needed.

Now we know that on the list in the Unwanted Guest Registry we can find demons, LHS's, evil spirits (those are LHS's under assignment), foul birds, imps, celestial beings, even an orifice serpent thing we saw recently. Some of these probably fall under a Leviathan kingdom, but like a boa constrictor (or a python) versus a snake versus a serpent versus a cobra versus an adder. We have seen them in our dealings.

We often looked at the creatures discussed in the book of Job as being figurative or allegorical, but Job was never allegorical. He was really telling us what it was.

We just ignored it. David did the same thing. The miry clay is a place. The pit is a place just like the Many Waters is a court...a courtroom. We have been in that court. We have also been in the Aquatic Court. We simply have not been tutored on the water courts and water kingdoms—yet.

As we discussed these things, we had an inkling that future engagements with Heaven would uncover information about these things.

———·———

Chapter 11

If You Build It, They Will Come

A common thread that we may have already experienced is that once we are aware of the concept of LHS's, they seem to find us. When we realize the redemptive work of helping LHS's transition to their destiny in Heaven, it fills us with awe and wonder at the goodness of God. I am always reminded that the Father wants to populate Heaven, not hell, and we get to cooperate with Heaven in ushering the millions of LHS's home.

One friend who works in this area found the smoke alarm in the home he was renovating would sound the alarm as if a fire was occurring. This was a battery-operated smoke alarm that had *no* batteries. This occurred time after time. It did not take him long to inquire as to the presence of an LHS when this would happen. The answer was always in the affirmative, so he would take the time to help usher them to Heaven.

Often, LHS's will utilize the things in our home or vehicle to alert us to their presence. Sometimes what they do can be quite annoying, but we must realize they are desperate to have a change of surroundings and simply want to go home.

We have experienced things happening to our vehicles that were unexplainable and usually undiagnosable. In the first book, I talk about ways they manifest and clues to look for when sensing or suspecting the presence of LHS's. It might be good to review that from time to time.

Many who work in this arena have found large numbers of LHS's in their realms, their homes, businesses, etc. Rather than being upset about, we need to realize 1) that they are persons, 2) they simply want to go home, and 3) if they are under demonic assignment, they probably are not under assignment willingly and desire to be freed of that assignment.

Reception Areas

Several colleagues who work with LHS's have found it beneficial to set up reception areas for them to gather in prior to being helped to transition. These reception areas vary in size and style, but have been helpful to keep them together prior to ministry to them.

The Green Room

One colleague has setup a Green Room for LHS's that (in life) were well-known. The Green Room provides a gathering place that provides privacy to them and aids their willingness to cooperate during their eventual transition.

The Catholic Hall

A colleague was led to build (in the spirit) a gathering place for those of the Catholic faith. Since Catholicism has certain rituals that are important to them, in some cases an LHS of that persuasion was not able to have Last Rites administered to them. In this room, that desire is accommodated prior to their transition.

The Hotel

Stephanie[13] was having so many encounters with LHS's that she found it necessary to ask Heaven to construct a hotel for all the LHS's she was dealing with. Like the other accommodations mentioned, she will check to see the occupancy level of the hotel and every few days will meet with the guests and help them make the transition.

In several of these gathering areas, they room is equipped, often with the sound of Adina's music, as well

---

[13] Stephanie is my Executive Assistant.

as a magazine called, "Your Destiny in Heaven", along with Living Water, and Bread of Life. All these accommodations are simply to make their stay more pleasant as they await their opportunity to transition.

We may wish to do something similar. Simply inquire in Heaven about what should be done and engage their assistance in building in the spirit what Heaven has instructed. Check with Heaven that we have the authority to build the structure in that location.

———·———

Chapter 12

Recognizing the Person

Recently, a wonderful lesson was learned by a colleague concerning the personhood of LHS's and how they deserve to be honored and respected. As she engaged Heaven, she discovered there were two LHS's and a demonic guard. One of them she knew was a boy, a young man, probably 20. He was tall and thin. She knew his name was Max and he just wanted relief. He simply wanted to go home. The other LHS, she did not even entertain. My colleague had experienced a tiring day and simply wanted to get this engagement over with. She was helping a friend through this process.

Concerning the second LHS, she made no inquiry if it was a male or female, none of that.

I will let my colleague tell the story:

I said to my friend that I was working with, 'You know, I really don't really care who this other one is. We're just going to go on and send them home.'

Suddenly, a woman presented herself to me. She was taking a step to go into the silver channel, and she turned and looked at me and she said, 'Why wouldn't you care what my name is? I'm a person, too.' She spoke in a very matter of fact manner and was genuinely hurt by my response. It caught me off guard and I said, 'You are right. I am deeply sorry.' Because in that moment I knew I had judged her because she had had a demonic guard. She extended her arm out to me and on her forearm, was a huge gash. She said, 'I did not want to do anything to hurt this person, but they made me.'

I was like, 'I will never judge another LHS again because they have a demonic guard.' You tend to want to think, 'Oh, they're evil, too. But they are not.'

On another occasion a ministry team was dealing with an LHS who had been hiding behind another. The second LHS did not present himself as evil (or under demonic assignment). The team had the sense that the first LHS had done evil all his life, however the second person had not lived that way. The one with the evil bend was reluctant to transition to Heaven until the team leader had a revelation that the first LHS had been severely abused by his father as a child. Suddenly, the team leader had a great deal of compassion toward that LHS. When the leader acknowledged his compassion toward the LHS, he was able to witness the LHS completely surrender. The leader remarked how they had never watched the full surrender of someone right before they step over into Heaven—someone who was angry and bitter. It was so good to see.

———·———

Chapter 13

Red & Black Capture Bags

The next several chapters are included in this book because they have relevance when ministering to LHS's. They are from my book, Dealing Trusts & Consequential Liens in the Courts of Heaven. *They deal with a tool/weapon known as capture bags that angels use in behalf us as sons and on behalf of the Kingdom.*

Stephanie and I had engaged Heaven and Ezekiel[14] appeared carrying a red bag. Knowing that things like colors are not accidental in Heaven, we asked about it. We were told it was a capturing bag and that he had captured an infiltration. He did not expound on that.

He wanted to teach us about capture bags, so we welcomed his instruction. The capturing bags are very

---

[14] Ezekiel is the Chief Angel assigned to LifeSpring.

important to be released and commissioned to the angels. The size of them matters. Begin to see, as we release capturing bags, the various sizes. There will be different sizes for different means. The one Ezekiel was carrying was a large size, because he dealt with a large infiltration, and it was necessary and needed for this specific capture. There are other capturing bags that will be of different colors. Each one of the various colors represents not only a color, but a size, depending upon the capture needed. Equip the angels with all the sizes. They are representative of a specific task, and it is what they use for specific captures.

The red bag, representing having the blood of Jesus infused in it, was needed and necessary to keep the capture of the infiltration Ezekiel was carrying.

Once they have captured the infiltration, they will destroy it along with the bag. There is a never-ending supply of the different sizes that represent the colors of the bags. Within the bag one could see what appeared to be a grid keeping the infiltration in the bag.

Ezekiel explained that it was part of the dismantling that is taking place on the earth today. These capturing bags are not new to angels, but they are new to us, especially regarding the different sizes and their meanings. He pointed out that this will be an important part that the ecclesia/the people will need to understand while commissioning their angels. It's a tool.

This will be an important part that the ecclesia/the people will need to understand while commissioning their angels. They are considered classifications in Heaven. There are some that are classifications for small demons—things that are easily captured or easily contained. Then there are some that are classified specifically for domains. It will capture a whole domain. This is where the fun begins when capturing domains.

An aspect of the authority that we have through Jesus to commission angels is the capturing of these domains—the collapsing of these domains. Other angels will be around with other classifications of these capturing bags, capturing the entities trying to flee. This is a part of a strategy of Heaven given to the saints to walk in freedom—to walk in their freedom and victory."

At this stage of learning we were told to commission with the angels with the classifications. Request all the classifications of the capture bags. We would soon learn about the different classifications that are represented as colors. He explained that the red one is one of the larger ones and it was not the one for domains, but it was used for infiltrations.

Capture Bag Commission

Ezekiel reminded us that the enemy would continue to try to infiltrate. That is why the classification of these bags is so important and the commissioning of the angels is so important. The people's commissioning of their angels with these is so important. It will prevent the infiltration into their own lives.

Worm holes are a type of infiltration. The capturing bags are things angels use as a tool—as a part of the dismantling of those infiltrations.

Angelic Commissioning

[Feel free to modify this commissioning for your angels and your situation.]

I call Ezekiel, his commanders, and his ranks, along with my angels to come near.

Father, I request on behalf of the angels, all the different sizes, classifications, and colors of every capturing bag needed to serve the Kingdom of Heaven and to serve your people, in Jesus' name.

Ezekiel, I commission you, your commanders, and your ranks to use the classifications of every capturing bag needed; to go and capture the infiltrations; to use the different colors and classifications of the bags as needed from the smallest demon to the largest domain, in the name of Jesus; to use these capturing bags throughout our realms and over LifeSpring, Sandhills Ecclesia, CourtsNet, and the other facets of LifeSpring, along with those that are at work on behalf of these ministries and for their families, in Jesus' mighty name.

He instructed us to include their families because this was a type of covering.

Immediately we saw Ezekiel with his arms loaded with various colors and sizes of capture bags. Within seconds he left to make use of the bags. With that, Ezekiel was finished with this brief training on capture bags.

Black Capture Bags

Stephanie and I were in a classroom engaging with Ezekiel, when he began to teach on black capture bags which are used for witchcraft. As we know, witchcraft is prominent in the land, and many people are used in witchcraft. The exploration of witchcraft is ancient and its usefulness to people is so misleading. It so captivates their hearts to darkness. This black capturing bag is significant, where the realms of darkness are used for sorcery, witchcraft, Luciferianism,[15] and Satanism.

When these bags are presented to the people, we can understand that there has been witchcraft at work, but the capturing of these things is easy. We plunder this regularly. Infiltrations of witchcraft, sorcery, Luciferianism, and Satanism will all be easily captured in these bags. Use them. They are our tools.

When we have been alerted that there have been possible infiltrations of witchcraft, sorcery, and the like, these are the tools angels will use. They will capture them. However, these bags are not for gathering plunder. Other bags are used for plunder.

---

[15] The worship of Lucifer is the aim of Freemasonry.

———·———

Chapter 14

Silver & Gold Capture Bags

A few days after seeing our first capture bag, Stephanie and I stepped into Heaven to learn some more about them. We were taken to an office, and the first thing Stephanie noticed was the color of the walls, which were golden-yellow.

Golden Glory Bags

Lydia[16] came to instruct us. She began to teach on what she called the gold glory bags. The color of the walls where we were was symbolic of how glory presents itself to the human eye. She explained that there were capturing bags and there were bags of Glory. These can be administered by the angels into people's realm.

---

[16] Lydia is a woman in white who advises our ministry.

Stephanie visualized us taking these bags and stepping into them and pulling them up around us. What Holy Spirit is showing me that we are doing is because the Glory is all encompassing. It surrounds us. These are like how we would release Godly bonds to people. It is something that we can release on behalf of people.

The Glory bags will be something that we commission their angels to bring to them.

It is a part of awakening their angels, stirring them up, working on behalf of those that come for prayer and for ministry.

Silver Capture Bags

A few days later we were in another engagement and found ourselves back in the ballroom we had seen in a different engagement.[17] This time we were to learn about silver bags. Malcolm[18] appeared and described how this bag was aerodynamic, but that it did not capture—rather, it contained. It contains something to be released to others. It contains the essence of the Father—the essence of Holy Spirit; and what it contains will bring the evidence of that into people's lives—the essence of the

---

[17] This is discussed in *Dealing with Trusts & Consequential Liens in the Courts of Heaven*, LifeSpring Publishing (2022).

[18] Malcolm is a man in white who often tutors us.

Father, the strength of the Father, the goodness of the Father, the plans of the Father, the need of the Father, the value of worship of the Father, and the friendship of the Father. These are necessary things that people have been missing in their lives. The use of these bags is also for the generations and is used in generational work.

Its usefulness is to capture the captive—those that are captive.

The Essence of the Father

Many like the simplicities and the simplistic ways that they can utilize tools of the Kingdom. That is what these bags are. People can mentally and visually speak and see these things as a helpful tool on their behalf because of the simplicity of it. When people are praying about it, it creates a boldness, a feeling of accomplishment, a sense of the co-laboring, and that they are useful in the co-laboring with the angels. They are gaining strength from it, and they are seeing results."

These are not capturing bags in the sense most of the other bags are. They are bags that *contain* the essence—all those things mentioned above to be given to that person. It acts like a bonding agent—like a bond. It can be a bond that is released when it is relevant and an opportune time to do so.

The usefulness of these silver bags comes when they are praying on behalf of someone, have them say, 'As an act of faith take that silver bag to myself.' Many have missed the relational side of prayer, but many can visually experience the relationship. They can physically experience the relationship of the Father as this tool is used by the body. This unsophisticated action shows the simplicity of Heaven, yet it is profound love and favor for the body and for the people. Think of it as an act of love, and in turn, our release of that on behalf of someone else is also an act of love—love for our neighbor, love for our friend, love for family, love for the Body of Christ.

Use this diligently. Use it often. The essence of the Father and His love will settle upon the people. There will be a fragrance about it—an enhancement because of it, a beauty around it, and a just cause will bear witness from it. Use this in our courtroom work. It is tangible. Its immediate effects will be known as the effective fervent prayers of a righteous man will avail much."[19]

We can simply receive the silver bags into our realms. It is tangible. This is something we can release to a believer who is struggling. It is very much like how a bond works.

The definition of essence is helpful to understand. Malcolm said, "It's an entire world." We took a moment to look at the definition of "essence."[20] It is quite interesting. "The intrinsic nature or indispensable

---

[19] James 5:16

[20] Google's English Dictionary definition of essence

quality of something that determines its character, especially something abstract."

The philosophy definition was, "The inherent unchanging nature of a thing or class of things, especially as contrasted with its existence", and also "a property or group of properties of something without which it would not exist or be what it is." An additional definition said, "An extract or concentrate obtained from a particular plant or other matter and used for flavoring or scent. It creates a frequency."

"The most significant element, quality, or aspect of a thing or person in concentrated form or substance as of a perfume."

"Something that exists, an entity."

Wikipedia had an interesting definition. "Essence. It's a polysomic term using philosophy and theology as a designation for the property or set of properties **that make an entity or substance what it fundamentally is** and which it has by necessity and **without which it loses its identity**."[21] (Emphasis added)

This essence can be released for those who do not understand this prayer paradigm, who need the Essence of the Father, His love, His friendship, and it will be astounding to them. They will experience a drawing near

---

[21] Wikipedia definition of essence

to the Father. We can simply receive the contents of the silver bag and holding the Glory bag into our realms.

Containers to be Released

They are containers to be released as opposed to bags that capture things. These two bags (gold and silver) are containers of the Glory of the Father and the Essence and Love of the Father that need to be released to people.

They are also containers to gather. We will utilize them to gather people into the Glory and the Essence and Love of the Father. Sometimes people who get caught up in words, when they are hearing people talk about the Glory, they have not ascertained how to utilize it for themselves. This is a simplistic, loving way that people can use their imaginations to utilize it for themselves and as they pray for others. We can also request these bags be released on behalf of LHS's. The Glory bag simply contains the Glory of God to be released to people.

Those who struggle when they hear these messages, and are falsely believing that they themselves cannot ascertain the Glory or ascertain the love and the Essence of the Father, these are great tools for them on their behalf. They *can* imagine. They *can see* whether they are a seer or not and can understand what a bag looks like, feels like, and *can* imagine themselves stepping into the Glory with the use of the tool that is the Glory bag. They *can* ascertain the essence and the experience of it with the tool that is the silver bag. Simplicity is needed at times, and at times these tools are needed.

Make skillful use of them for they are for our benefit because of the Father's love. Because we have said yes to co-laboring with angels, this is a direct result and a benefit of that. It is a reminder that angels are not just useful in battle, but they are useful in the presentation of the Father's love and of His Glory and of His Kingdom."

We can commission Angels to take the silver bags to those who have drawn near the ministry we were told. The benefit of these bags to the people has been a great honor to deliver on behalf of those that have drawn close to the ministry and especially on behalf of those who work for the ministry. It is the Father's love.

Great benefit comes from loving the Father and choosing His Kingdom.

These are Kingdom benefits. Look at them like that. Teach the people Kingdom benefits. Align ourselves with the Kingdom of Heaven. As simple as this may seem, it will work profoundly in our lives for the Father smiles down upon this ministry.

The Essence *and* the Glory

As revelation unfolded, we had another engagement in which we saw a picture of what the Essence and the Glory look like together—a pure white light. The light then leapt off the table and into outer space.

We were told by Joseph, a man in white that the Father's Glory and Essence upon the earth upon men's hearts and upon their realms, would be evident just as we see the flame, just as in the day when Holy Spirit came, and flames were seen above the people.[22] The essence will rest upon the people.

We were invited to walk with him, and we stopped at a brook, and referring to an engagement David, Stephanie, and I had the prior day, said, "The baptismal pool we saw is an invitation to not just to Sandhills Ecclesia,[23] but to all who draw close to the ministry, to step into the water which contains the Essence of His Glory—there will be evidence upon their lives. We will see the evidence. This is the goodness of Heaven. The early believers experienced the evidence of speaking a language heretofore unknown to them. Heaven is going to do this marvelous thing.

We were then transported back to a different room. Jason, a man in white, was present to assist us. He brought an ancient book. On the cover was a large medallion and Jason took a sword and inserted it into the keyhole that was in the medallion and turned the sword like a key. As he did, one could hear the unlocking of the lock mechanism. The book was entitled, *The Book of Numbers*. Stephanie asked if this was "a" book of numbers, or "the" [Biblical] book of Numbers. She was assured it was the latter, and it was suggested we turn to

---

[22] Acts 2:3

[23] Sandhills Ecclesia is a weekly gathering of believers via Zoom to legislate in the earth. (See SandhillsEcclesia.com). This message is dated 2/27/22 and is available on the website.

Numbers 4. Jason began helping unpack information in that passage and later in chapter 27, which spoke of inheritance. A principle of inheritance was unveiled that is simply:

An inheritance may be distributed, but to have benefit, it must be possessed.

The passage in Numbers 27 spoke of those who were to carry the presence. Today, that is us.

Each of our realms carries the tabernacle within us.[24] We are a type and shadow of the tabernacle, the holy that lives within us—the Essence AND the Glory we carry within us. There are those in need that need this Essence and this Glory. It will shine and be evident upon each of us. They will see it. They will know it. They will want it and desire it.

This is confirmed in 1 Peter 2:5-7:

> *⁵ Come and be His 'living stones' who are continually being assembled into a sanctuary for God. For now, you serve as holy priests, offering up spiritual sacrifices that He readily accepts through Jesus Christ. ⁶ For it says in Scripture:*

---

[24] 1 Corinthians 6:19 "Have you forgotten that your body is now the sacred temple of the Spirit of Holiness, who lives in you? You don't belong to yourself any longer, for the gift of God, the Holy Spirit, lives inside your sanctuary." (TPT); also 2 Corinthians 6:19

Look! I lay a cornerstone in Zion, a chosen and priceless stone! And whoever believes in Him will certainly not be disappointed. ⁷ As believers you know His great worth—indeed, **His preciousness is imparted to you.** *But for those who do not believe: The stone that the builders rejected and discarded has now become the cornerstone. (TPT) (Emphasis mine)*

The flame that people see upon us will be so evident that many will be drawn to it, and it will alight upon others.

This is a fulfillment of what Isaiah spoke of long ago:

¹ Arise, shine; for your light has come! And the glory of the LORD is risen upon you. ² For behold, the darkness shall cover the earth, and deep darkness the people; but the LORD will arise over you, and His glory will be seen upon you.

³ The Gentiles shall come to your light, and kings to the brightness of your rising. ⁴ "Lift up your eyes all around, and see: they all gather together, they come to you; your sons shall come from afar, and your daughters shall be nursed at your side. ⁵ Then **you shall see and become radiant***, and your heart shall swell with joy; because the abundance of the sea shall be turned to you, the wealth of the Gentiles shall come to you. (Isaiah 60:1-5) (Emphasis mine)*

All that we were hearing was referring to the baptism of Holy Spirit *and* fire. The Essence and the Glory is what creates the fire. The fire is the Essence *and* the Glory combined.

Imagine the two of them together—the gold and the silver bags. When we release these for people and on behalf of people, contained within them and combined is the fire.

> *Moses brought their case before the Lord. ⁶ And the Lord spoke to Moses saying ⁷ the daughters of Zelophedad speak what is right; you shall surely give them a possession of inheritance among their father's brothers, and cause the inheritance of their father to pass to them. (Numbers 27:5)*

Just like in Numbers 27 where the Lord laid out what inheritances were for the people on our earth, this is an inheritance. This is the truest form of inheritance from the Father—His Glory and His Essence combined, bringing the fire upon the people, lighting the fire within them, dwelling upon them, and being so evident that people are drawn to the light—the flame.

In the beginning, when the Lord set up the inheritance in the natural using the Courts of Heaven, there is also an inheritance for us in the spiritual. Here it not only has to be distributed, but this inheritance also *must be possessed*. The sword of the Lord—it is our strength and Wisdom[25] is at our right hand. The Glory and the Essence that will be upon us brings the fire of the Lord.

On behalf of this ministry, this was a new walk—a new beginning for the people and for the Kingdom, with new insight and new understanding—all gained from the seat of rest all of it because He loves us.

Heaven said, "This flame will be evident upon us just as it is evident in my hand. As the Father releases His Glory and His Essence upon the people, and what we described as an ember will be a movement."

This is what the earth groans for. An innumerable number of angels carry this. They carry this torch. They carry this flame which is being released for such a time as this. It will grow just as a natural fire grows and will spread. This will spread. This will bring people from the north, south, east, and west.

The Commission for the Essence & the Glory[26]

I commission you in the name of Jesus, Ezekiel, with your commanders, and ranks on behalf of the people, those who have drawn near to the ministry, those who work for the ministry, and their families, to bring the flame that is the Essence and the Glory of the Father upon the

---

[25] Wisdom is a heavenly entity, one of the seven spirits of God.

[26] Feel free to customize this to your situation.

people that it spread like embers and light upon the people so that all may see that it as evidence, as the Father has said that it would be in evidence.

I commission you to the full use of the silver and the gold bags that carry the Essence and carry the Glory and to bring them to everyone's realms in the name of Jesus.

Father, I would like for Understanding to go with this commissioning that is being released—this fire.

Father, I request that Understanding be released for all of those that hear, that draw near, that seek the Kingdom of God, and I release you, Ezekiel, your commanders, and ranks to do this good work on behalf of the Father, in Jesus' name.

I commission you to these things both in time and out of time.

With that, Ezekiel turned and left.

Welcoming Understanding

We were told that much understanding would come from this. We were to be patient. This is a new level. A new place. Understanding will come. Understanding is going to be playing a very large role at this level.

We welcomed Understanding saying, "I welcome you in everything; and just like I hold Wisdom's hand, I want to hold your hand."

There are new frequencies being released upon the earth through these messages; frequencies that are so supernatural, that Understanding being released upon them is what is going to bring this understanding of this frequency to their ears. Just like the flame and the embers, we will see it grow among the people quickly.

———·———

Chapter 15

Purple Capture Bags

Purple was the color of the capture bag we would be learning about in this engagement with Heaven.

Other Times & Dimensions

We noted a change in the wall color as we had in other engagements. This time they switched to purple—a deep purple. It was very beautiful, and it had flashes of light through it, all over the walls like there were mirrors on the walls reflecting light. This deep royal purple was the next step down from the red capture bags. The purple bag goes into *dimensions*. It is what is needed and useful when going into other times and dimensions. It prevents what is captured from escaping when angels are taking them out of other times and dimensions. It is lined with the authority that is interwoven into the fabric of the bag, but it is a grid. It is a very useful tool. As we know, Ezekiel told us they will be doing many things *in time and out of time* and this is the purpose of this specific capturing bag.

When we commission our angels, we are to use the full commissioning of a capturing bag of every size, color, and dimension. (We were rapidly progressing in our understanding of how to commission our angels concerning the capture bags.

The blood is upon all the bags, the Name above all names, and the authority of that name is upon all of them. The colors are for our knowledge and understanding. we will see them play out as we work in this paradigm of prayer using these capturing bags. We will know specifically when angels come with a specific color bag what has been captured, whether it's an infiltration, whether it's black for witchcraft, or whether it's this deep, royal purple which is where something was caught in a different time, age, and dimension for our knowledge. This is the wisdom of Heaven and because of the Father's love for us, He wants us to know all these things.

———·———

Chapter 16

Green & Blue Capture Bags

Continuing the prior engagement, the room suddenly changed colors to green. Ezekiel explained, "These are the plunder bag colors. The green represents the wealth, and the sevenfold return of things stolen. *We can use them in tandem as we plunder the kingdoms of darkness.*"

Green Capture Bags

We were told that we were to receive this information because the Father loves the authority that we stand in and the co-laboring with angels that we do. The Angels of the Hosts have not been nearly as active as Heaven wants them to be, but the saints are awakening to them and their work. He gives this information because He loves this—the awakening of His children, the hunger for knowledge, the hunger for Heaven, the hunger for Him. It is His great pleasure. It is His joy.

The lessons in leaning in our paradigms of prayer was for when we call upon the angels to use these capturing bags during times of attack, especially the release of the Glory bags for the people. They work in tandem when we call upon the angels to silence the principalities. The end-product of this is the usefulness with the angels and the co-laboring with the saints and the use of the capturing bags, and the Glory bags and the silver bags. They produce a quick silencing of the enemy, and the opening of the Kingdom dynamics of Heaven.

Our realms, who we are, how God created us, our arche[27] that we have learned about, which also includes mountains—even things we don't understand—it is a landscape, which is why the principalities consider it a region. Which is why it is impacted by a consequential lien.[28]

Our footsteps on the earth create our region upon the earth.

We were shown a brilliantly shining bright orb hovering over the table in the conference room. On the table were four books: the Book of LifeSpring, the Book of Sandhills Ecclesia, the Book of CourtsNet, and the BAS

---

[27] See my book *Kingdom Dynamics* (LifeSpring Publishing (2022).

[28] Consequential liens are discussed in *Dealing with Trusts & Consequential Liens in the Courts of Heaven*, LifeSpring Publishing (2022).

Global[29] book were on the table. The orb was the light of what was coming. As the orb came closer to the table, it grew in mass. It hovered above all four books. Power was going into *all* the books, but was also hovering above them. We were told it was knowledge, integrity, wisdom—a lightning-force swift action upon the hearts of man that come into this teaching, it was Kingdom dynamics because we pray 'Your Kingdom come, Your will be done,' it was His ultimate will. That's what this orb was—His will. We were told we could think of it in those terms. Many aspects to what we were seeing came out of this as His will. It is because the Kingdom is at hand.

We came to understand that because of obedience, prayer, and all the things Heaven had been showing us, that His will was evident in all four of the books. It is a pouring out of all those things mentioned in those books that will affect the people as it reflects the ministry, which reflects His will because of praying for His Kingdom to come.[30]

Everyone one who had joined us began leaving the room, but the books were still open. We were shown that another book was coming. We had seen the books for LifeSpring, CourtsNet, BAS Global, and Sandhills

---

[29] BAS (Business Advocate Services), now known as Heaven Down Business, is an extension of LifeSpring.

[30] For years I have prayed, "Come Kingdom of God, be done will of God" in my daily prayer life.

Ecclesia, but the new book was more darkened and not opened yet. Apparently, its content is still to be unveiled.

The Commissioning[31]

I call Ezekiel, his commanders, and his ranks, along with my angels to come near. Father, I request on behalf of the angels, all the different sizes, classifications, and colors of every capturing bag needed to serve the Kingdom of Heaven and to serve your people, in Jesus' name.

Ezekiel, I commission you, your commanders, and your ranks to use the classifications of every capturing bag needed to go and capture the infiltrations, to use the different colors and classifications of the bags as needed from the smallest demon to the largest domain, in the name of Jesus.

I also request of the Father Glory bags for distribution to the saints hearing this message as well as silver bags.

I commission you to the full use of these gold Glory bags and the silver bags for the Glory of the Father in the lives of His sons and daughters, in Jesus' name.

---

[31] Feel free to adapt this commissioning to your situation.

Blue Capture Bags

We had seen blue capture bags but had no understanding of them. We were desiring instruction about the blue capture bags, which typically appeared much smaller—more of a regular size than some other capture bags we had seen. Malcolm explained to us that the blue bags capture the enemy's weapons.

Satan is a legalist, but he is also a copycat. His falsehood presents weaponry as we would, in the natural think of weaponry, but his weapons *are only **tactics***. This has perplexed us in that, in the natural, we think of him attacking us with weapons. His weapons are *words* and *lies—tactical strategies of deception*. The blue bags capture the paradigms that perplex us.

When it comes to the enemy's warfare and talking about arrows, our armor will deflect the arrows from the enemy. We may have always assumed they were actual weapons. We saw them as actual arrows, but words or strategies can inflict more damage than a natural arrow ever could upon a person's realms. Capture the accusations! In this paradigm we don't have to get caught up in saying, "Angels, go and capture the words and the phrases and the strategies." We can say, "Capture the accusations." We can do that before the enemy has a legal right to bring it to the Courts of Heaven against us. This is the sovereignty of God on behalf of His sons.

Picture Jacob's ladder and how the accuser ascends and descends a ladder to bring accusations against us.

Sometimes, the enemy comes to us personally, speaking to us about where to accuse ourselves, or about where we accuse others in our hearts and our mind.

---

*To make an accusation
is not a sin until we embrace it
and we act upon it.*

This can be done to prevent those words and accusations of the enemy from reaching our spirit and our heart and our soul. Our repentance is for the entertaining of these accusations against others and against ourselves, et cetera. Before the enemy can take an accusation to the Courts of Heaven to accuse us and where we must come into agreement with the accuser, *the step before that* is when we come into agreement—we hear it, and we take it on. That is when he can have a legal right to accuse us.

The blue capture bags are a part of the paradigms of prayer to forfeit the enemy's legal right to form accusations against us. This is a gift from the Father. This bag is for is His sovereignty towards us in that if we can utilize this commissioning of the angels, it is a prevention of the next step of the enemy against us, which is where we would come into agreement or take on the accusation. It circumvents that for us *because we are His children*. The Father is the one who has simplified this aspect, so we are not dealing with accusations over and over repeatedly. Heaven is simply taking that out of the equation for us. Look how the Father loves. That is what this is. He is giving us this tool. It's like a preventative medicine.

It is for dismantling something before it begins. It's a preventative.

People have just been sick and tired of the same accusations over and over repeatedly. This tool is something we can use in our paradigms of prayer as we commission angels to use this on our behalf where we are not accepting or falling for the enemy's tactics but instead are being given Kingdom tactics that are offensive not defensive. It is for us preventative measures.

Hand in Hand with Wisdom

Wisdom appeared with a large iridescent pearl in her hand. She was turning it in her hand and reminded us that she had given us the Wisdom of Ages a few days before. She instructed us to tell the people to invoke her. She said, "Invoke Wisdom in *everything* that they do and in all the teachings that are being taught. If they come to her door, request Wisdom and the angels to use the capture bags along with the extraordinary things that LifeSpring brings to people, and that she will give them the Wisdom of Ages.

It is the Father's desire that we carry Wisdom—the Pearls of Wisdom around our neck. She then set a large Pearl of Wisdom on the table in front of me and said, "It is ours for the keeping. It's the continuing of the Wisdom of Ages. Teach the people that Wisdom must be invoked—she must be invited. It is necessary.

Walking Together

Ezekiel then appeared, demonstrating how he and Wisdom walk together through things. He was demonstrating that as we teach the people about Wisdom and the need to understand that using Wisdom and all these things, including arming our angels, co-laboring with our angels, that walking with the entity Wisdom is an important piece of the puzzle.

He has showed us that he and Wisdom were holding hands. That's how he wants the people to see themselves, as holding hands with Wisdom and Wisdom holding hands with Ezekiel. This is also a representation of their own personal angels who should be commissioned to walk hand in hand with Wisdom. It's a three-cord strand.

He smiled and began to walk away together with Wisdom. In his other hand he slung an orange bag over his shoulder.

> *6 Wisdom is a gift from a generous God, and every word Wisdom speaks is full of revelation and becomes a fountain of understanding within you.*
>
> *9 Then you will discover all that is just, proper, and fair, and be empowered to make the right decisions as you walk into your destiny.*

¹⁰ When Wisdom wins your heart and revelation breaks in, true pleasure enters your soul. (Proverbs 2:6, 9-10) (TPT)

Grey Capture Bags

Jeremy, one of our team members was in prayer recently in response to a request for how to deal with a situation he was facing in his home. Jeremy and his wife parent several small children and he noticed some movies or television shows were releasing a lot of profanity into the air which was polluting the atmosphere. He heard Heaven say, "Request grey capture bags."

Asking what they did, he heard, "The grey capture bags work much like a shop vac or leaf blower that has both sucking and blowing capabilities...they have dual use. When requesting the grey capture bags, essentially our angels will be able to kill 2 birds with one stone."

Heaven said, "The **first component is the isolation and removal of any ungodly frequencies.**" He could see an angel holding a bag that was fully inflated and it was sucking in all the ungodly frequencies in the space in front and around of where the bag was positioned.

Heaven continued, **"The second feature is the release of Godly frequencies and the frequency of Heaven."**

Again, he could see the angel with the bag, only this time a golden sparkling mist was being released.

He said, "It basically has dual-action cleaning power." My angel chuckled and then showed me how the ungodly frequencies can suck the life and joy out of an atmosphere and leave the people in that atmosphere feeling heavy or agitated.

He saw the scene depicting this as a vivid image that had all the color sucked out of it. The individuals in the image looked very melancholy but when the Godly frequencies were released it was like a revival breaking out, suddenly the color reappeared, more vibrant than before and everyone seemed alive with the joy of the Lord. There was also a serenity and a peace that came over the scene with the release of these Godly frequencies.

He sensed the need to request and commission his angels to use this new item for his house and family.

Father, in Jesus' name I request the grey capture bags for our angels and ranks and I commission our angels to use these bags to remove the ungodly frequencies and release the heavenly frequencies into our home and realms, in Jesus' name.

He asked, "Can these be used in tandem with other frequency weapons like shields and headphones. He heard, "Yes."

He asked, "Are they specifically for the frequencies of words and sound waves and again he heard, "Yes."

Adding the grey capture bags to the tool kit of Heaven known as capture bags should help the Body of Christ gain new levels of freedom. Enjoy them! Use them!

——— · ———

Chapter 17

Orange, Brown & Tan Capture Bags

Orange was the color for today. As Ezekiel was walking away in a prior engagement, we noticed he was carrying an orange bag over his shoulder.

Orange Capture Bags

Asking what it was about, Ezekiel paused and said, "It's for domains. **Orange is the capturing of a domain.** Domains are evil empires—evil domains. I used it in conjunction with the Purple bag. (We could see purple bag inside of the orange bag.) This domain that I captured was in another time and dimension."

Ezekiel had captured a domain—one that was encroaching upon the ministry that was being built by the enemy to create an illusion to other people—a false domain. Someone was trying to create a false domain to be a replica—a duplicate of LifeSpring Ministries, but he captured it. Remember, he takes these and destroys them *and* the bags. He would be taking this orange bag to destroy it. The domain Ezekiel spoke of was two-fold. (1) The domain where someone was going to duplicate or create a false replica of LifeSpring Ministries, where when people go to a search of LifeSpring, they were going to be taken to a different place. It was the false domain in the natural as well as (2) a domain in the spiritual—a room where it was created in a different dimension in time.

We thanked him for the capture, and he disclosed that the strategy for that capture had come from the Strategy Room. He knew from the Strategy Room where to go to capture this domain in time and out of time, as well as taking down that platform.

We again thanked Ezekiel as he walked away having taught us even more about capture bags and the various colors.

Brown Capture Bags

Earlier in the day I mentioned to Stephanie that I wanted to learn more about capture bags and more about what certain colors meant. We stepped into the realms of Heaven, asking for a meeting with Malcolm. He was waiting for us in the classroom with an eraser and two pieces of chalk in his hand.

When he asked what we wanted to learn about today, we responded with an answer that we felt he already knew. We wanted to know about the different color bags.

We heard the word "aerodynamic."

Malcolm told us we heard the word aerodynamic for a reason. It is their usefulness. In the natural when something is aerodynamic, it goes faster. Malcolm then began drawing on the whiteboard. He drew a big bag. The larger he drew it, the larger the whiteboard became. He became small in comparison. As he was drawing on the whiteboard, we could see the rope with which angels tie capture bags. It was a very large bag. He was going to talk to us about size and color simultaneously. With that, Malcolm began coloring the bag brown.

Dominions on Land

We learned that this brown bag **captures land that was taken captive by the enemy.** It is essentially 'illegal land', or land under an illegal ownership claim.

The vision we saw was of land taken captive by the enemy that belongs to the children of God—the sons of God. It was like a dominion but was not a dominion. This was taking captive a dominion that has been encamped and where the enemy had encroached upon the land. It was like a territory, but unlike the domains which can be captured in the Orange Bag, it is different from that because this one deals with physical earth. In the situation we were seeing it was the result of a consequential lien that a principality put upon a region of land or someone's land that was stolen. This was an encroaching of an evil dominion upon land.

We then saw where natural land had been cursed by the bloodshed that occurred on it and it had been stolen. The legal right was two-fold—the shedding of innocent blood, and the theft of the land. It gave the legal right to the principality to overlay an evil dominion on someone's territory or land mass in the natural.

Remember the account in the book of Daniel about princes being over regions—like the Prince of Persia being over a region that was an entire land mass. It contained an entire body of people. The freedom from them is for individuals' sakes and for families' sakes. This pertains to land that has been stolen from people, even in the natural. Think of it as the land that the Native Americans had stolen from them. An evil dominion has been placed over them and their heritage—an evil dominion that can be easily captured—easily dismantled.

Repentance work that has already been done concerning land that has been taken like that can be applied for the capture bags by simply commissioning the angels to retrieve the land and remove the captured principality. Other repentance work may also be needed. Be led of Holy Spirit in that arena.

The ability to remove the principality is a part of the parameter[32] and will be a useful tool when dealing with parameters that are seen on someone's life as a trust. The Godly trust in this is all that Heaven has for us including inheritances that were stolen from us—which includes land.

Stephanie desired an illustration of what Malcolm was telling us. She began to see Kevin (one of our Senior Advocates) doing courtroom work and looking at someone's Trust Registry, realizing that there is a parameter and a consequential lien that has been placed upon land that has been stolen geographically and people groups who live on that land. She exclaimed, "He is showing it to me as masses of people and I keep seeing Native Americans specifically.

In the vision we saw was a land mass—an actual natural land mass. We saw a coastline and a castle on a hill overlooking the ocean. We saw the whole land mass captured, then we saw the evil domain overlaying the captured land mass. The purpose of this brown capture bag, in use with consequential liens, is to capture the dominion and free the land mass. "Is it that easy to capture the dominion?" we asked Malcolm.

"Well, yes! This IS Heaven!" he exclaimed.

Instead of dealing with little peon demons, we are dealing with principalities and getting it over with. We

---

[32] Parameters are discussed in-depth in my book *Dealing with Trusts & Consequential Liens in the Courts of Heaven*, LifeSpring Publishing (2022).

are just now beginning to understand the magnitude of the finished work of Jesus with the simplicity of what we have as sons of God, because of His finished work and His blood that was shed. This is the work of Heaven and the Kingdom dynamics.

How does this work in relation to cities?

There are evil dominions who have taken over land masses and cities. Remember the Prince of Persia. As we are doing this work with the capture bags that are given to the angels it is like what was used by the angel that visited Daniel. That is what was used then and that is what will be used now—a brown capture bag."

Imagine individual capture bags that are brown related to every state of the United States. Imagine looking at each state in the natural and then see in the spirit the overlay of the evil dominion over each state, city, or town. Now see the bloodshed that has occurred over them. That is how the dominion can take authority.

One of the first things to look at concerning the legal right a prince exercises is innocent bloodshed and profane worship and all the things we have been taught related to this. That is why that information was the forerunner of understanding to this paradigm now.

Dominions on the Seas

Not only do we have evil dominions over land, but also over the seas. Envision the bloodshed on ships, some of whom were slaves or died in war, ships that went down into the seas which were related to the work of water kingdoms, and where the dominion had captured LHS's in that place. The work would be two-fold: dealing with the principality through repentance for the bloodshed, et cetera, and helping the LHS's get free and transition to Heaven.

We had a recent example of that when we did some repentance work for bloodshed in Mississippi and on the Mississippi River. David Porter (one of our team members) had seen a piece of the Mississippi river open and hundreds of LHS's set free. There is a correlation of dominions to water kingdoms that needs to be understood.

We asked if he had more to discuss about the brown capture bags. He showed Stephanie a picture of a little child trying to tie their shoelaces. It might take a few moments at first, but eventually we become very skilled at it. He said, "The work and the simplicity of tying a shoelace is the simplicity of this work."

Capturing Dominions

Stephanie could then see the brown capture bags. They were brought into the conference room and on these bags was written 'Vital Work' in white stitching on the brown bags. The capture of dominions is vital work.

Remember its simplicity. There will be detailed information given during times of prayer, corporate prayer, prayer over cities and nations, intercessory prayer where the full use of these vital works of capturing dominions will be used. There will be great freedom, atmospheric changes, landscape changes, mass movement—movement that is twofold—like a massive group of people moving and then the movement as an earthquake would bring to the shifting of land.

This is no light matter, but it is simplistic. Heaven will instruct because the power of the blood and the final work of Jesus have created this for mankind. The groaning of the earth has called out for such a time as this.

The Mass Release of LHS's

In a brief vision some of what we saw was on land, and when the brown capture bags were utilized, a freeing of LHS's that had been trapped in that evil dominion occurred. Hundreds and thousands can be freed through this work. There is a streamlining to that process for the mass release of LHS's which involves the use of the brown capture bags for dominions. The dominions have held them and have traded on them. The dominions have inflicted a seizure upon them.

In a short vision Stephanie saw a massive angel with a brown capture bag. He flew down with the bag and captured the dominion in it. Whereas before it appeared as if a dark film had been over the landscape, suddenly light came breaking through. It produced an atmospheric change that allowed the release of LHS's that had been in captivity because when we capture the dominion, we are not capturing the souls of people or the spirits of people, we are capturing the demonic principality. Yet, we are also freeing the LHS's and the souls or spirits of people.

The simplicity is in the capture.

The complexity is in knowing when and how to commission the angels. We were reminded of a recent scene like what we experienced with the Sandhills Ecclesia as we did courtroom work concerning Mississippi and Canada. At that time David[33] saw a segment of the Mississippi River with LHS's coming out of it and going through the silver channel.

Malcolm urged, "Taste and see that the Lord is good. More instruction will come. It will seem tedious at first, but it will become very natural to us to do this.

Someone again illustrated by showing a child learning to tie their shoe. At first it seemed difficult, but after some practice it became second nature, and we can do it without even thinking about it.

We could perceive that everyone we had seen during this engagement was very well pleased. They are glad that this work is going to be done.

We had seen many Warrior Angels outside the window of the conference room who were capturing

---

[33] David Porter III, Lead Apostle for Sandhills Ecclesia

angels. They are part of this work, they are simply waiting to be deployed, and they are waiting with great anticipation.

A passage of Scripture came to mind from Romans 8:

"[18] I am convinced that any suffering we endure is less than nothing compared to the magnitude of glory that is about to be unveiled within us. [19] The entire universe is standing on tiptoe, yearning to see the unveiling of God's glorious sons and daughters!

[20] For against its will the universe itself has had to endure the empty futility resulting from the consequences of human sin. But now, with eager expectation, [21] all creation longs for freedom from its slavery to decay and to experience with us the wonderful freedom coming to God's children. [22] To this day we are aware of the universal agony and groaning of creation, as if it were in the contractions of labor for childbirth. [23] And it's not just creation. We who have already experienced the first fruits of the Spirit also inwardly groan as we passionately long to experience our full status as God's sons and daughters—including our physical bodies being transformed.

[24] For this is the hope of our salvation. But hope means that we must trust and wait for what is still unseen. For why would we need to hope for something we already have? [25] So because our

hope is set on what is yet to be seen, we patiently keep on waiting for its fulfillment. (Romans 8: 18-25)

What this brown capture bag talks about are those things where our sin brought us into the captivity—that includes lingering spirits and their activity. We were in awe because we were seeing this ancient text played out now!

Our obedience in the toughness of the LHS book release when we walked through what could have been fear as we released that book—the consequence of that will be the mass release of LHS's as people walk in this and in co-labor with Heaven and with angels. There had to be a beginning.

Tan Capture Bags

Stephanie and I had engaged Heaven regarding more information on the capture bags. Ezekiel, who met us, explained that we need not assume the possibility that there is every color of bag available to do different things in the spirit. There are some we may not yet ever know what the color is, but the usefulness of the bags is available on behalf of the people's angels to have full use of. There are dynamics of the use of every bag.

The bag he was holding looked like camel hair, a tan color. Angels use them in *correlation with* the domain bags (orange bags) and in *conjunction with* the domain bags. They are very specific to domains, not in an inclusive way of just what we think of as domains within websites, but domains of the enemy. There is treachery in domains and heresy in domains.

This bag does not so much capture, rather it is used to lay down upon the treachery, upon the heresy that is in those domains, covering it. Think of it as a trampling. We lay them down and we use them in that manner. The usefulness of it as a trampling upon the domains as we go and capture domains, we lay it down, ahead of the treachery or on top of the treachery. Angels lay it on the treachery and the heresy. The heresy Ezekiel was speaking of is an actual, tangible thing—not just a word or a deed. Heresies create structures. Angels trample down the heresy and the treachery with the use of this bag.

This can clearly be applied where occultism is involved. The foundation of occultism is heresy. It is treachery. The bags provide a covering where our feet can land securely as we go into a place as a conquering son. As we've read in the Bible, where our feet tread upon the adder and the lion, and our feet tread upon the serpent and the snake,[34] this is like that!

When there is a snake, we are supposed to throw a blanket over it or throw something over it and stomp on it. That is what I just saw Ezekiel do! Ezekiel reminded us that the understanding of these bags is for our purposes

---

[34] Psalm 91:13

to know *what* they are conquering. It is a way in which we can understand how the commissioning can be done.

> *I commission that these bags be laid out before you as you tread upon the lion and the adder, as you tread upon the scorpion and the snake, for these to be laid out before you as you co-labor. As you walk in the victories, THAT is the full use, Ezekiel.*
>
> *Ezekiel, I commend you to the Father. You, your ranks, and your commanders, and I commission you, your commanders, and ranks with the full use of this bag, to lay it down before the people, to lay it down upon the treachery—upon the heresy. As I move forward, co-laboring with you, I can walk and tread upon the lion and the adder, to tread upon the scorpion and the snake; to tread upon those things with victory, commissioning you to do this in full use of all the other bags, in time and out of time, and in every realm and dimension. I seal this with the blood of Jesus and the Sword of the Lord. I thank you.*
>
> *I thank you, Father, that you keep showing me how You go before me, preparing every way.*

Describing what she was now seeing, Stephanie said, "I'm seeing Ezekiel snatching up things using black bags. I'm seeing him using the purple bags right now. He has laid down those bags before him. I'm watching him with domains, capturing with the orange bags. It's as if I'm seeing the way in which the enemy has put together their use of infiltrations into domains using occultism and all of that together. This is just such a complete picture of that."

Stephanie continued, "I could only see Ezekiel from his knees down, and he had this armor on his feet. His angels were throwing the tan camel hair looking bag down ahead of them. It was, if we think of that movie years ago, *Raiders of the Lost Ark* with Harrison Ford, the one where he went into the temples and there were snakes all over the ground—it was like that. I was seeing the angels cast these out in front of them, and it covered the snakes. Then, as they were walking, I could hear the crunching of the snakes underneath of their feet."

———·———

Chapter 18

Pink Capture Bags

Stephanie and I had engaged Heaven and we were in a boardroom with Malcolm. We had questions about some of the colors of bags others had seen and had asked me about.

Pink Capture Bags

On the whiteboard, Malcolm drew a pink bag and said it was for capturing innocence that has been stolen. This, too, is an *in time and out of time* revelation. Just as a newborn arrives with innocence, and the purity that that brings within a newborn, there is still deep corruption in the DNA and RNA, even at birth, even though they appear innocent. That is why this is used in time and out of time.

> *The innocence that was stolen in the generational line can be brought to bear.*

It can be restored to the person or to the family line. As angels bring the innocence that was stolen back into the heavenly realms—as people step into Heaven, Innocence[35] will greet them.

The vision we had was of Innocence as a piece of themselves greeting them and enveloping them, restoring the innocence that was taken from them—from their RNA and from their DNA. It becomes as a covering upon their realms—like a garment.

The reason this is given in Heaven is because this is where Innocence stands.

> *And He chose us to be His very own, joining us to Himself even before He laid the foundation of the universe! Because of His great love, He ordained us, so that we would be seen as holy in His eyes with* ***an unstained innocence.*** *(Ephesians 1:4) (TPT) (Emphasis added)*

It brings wholeness back to their soul or their spirit as a covering.

---

[35] Innocence is a heavenly entity.

*[19] For God is satisfied to have all His fullness dwelling in Christ. [20] And by the blood of His cross, everything in heaven and earth is brought back to Himself—back to its original intent, **restored to innocence again!** [21-22] Even though you were once distant from Him, living in the shadows of your evil thoughts and actions, **He reconnected you back to Himself.** He released His supernatural peace to you through the sacrifice of His own body as the sin-payment on your behalf so that you would dwell in His presence. And now there is nothing between you and Father God, for He sees you as holy, flawless, and restored.... (Colossians 1:19-22) (TPT)*

Someone steps into Heaven who has asked for this innocence to be brought back to them or to a family member. When they step into Heaven it is like they are greeted by it. I saw a greeting like 'Hello, Stephanie!' and an acknowledgement. 'Hello innocence.' It became like a garment. It was put on like a robe over their whole being.

Restoring Innocence

What is the procedure to use this for restoring innocence?

Repentance for the generational line for participating or being a part of the corruption that steals the innocence—the stolen innocence from the ages.

If it is our spirit man in Heaven and Innocence greets us there, this is the truest understanding of living spirit forward. Our spirit man wears Innocence as a garment and brings it to the soul and to the body. *It is a calling of it back to us w*ith the understanding that because of the finished work, the complete work that Jesus did, we can call back the innocence of our RNA and DNA. We can bring it from our spirit man to our soul, then it comes to the body. It is a co-laboring of our spirit man and our soul and our body, too. Heaven has perfected what co-laboring means. They have been showing us over the last while the co-laboring of the angels with us.

Recently, they have shown us the co-laboring that will be between us and each other as we walk through this. Now they are showing us the co-laboring of our spirit, soul, and body. This is a labor of love from the Father.

In doing this on behalf of our generations, as we do this work with Freemasonry, Mithraism, and other things with calling this Innocence back to ourselves, how will this affect the next generation?

This is part of the finished work of Jesus.

As we walk through the realms of Heaven, we can do this on behalf of people with the authority that we carry.

We can stir up someone's spirit man, that is asleep. All the downloads from Heaven from the Godly bonds that are released upon people's realms is, in fact, a stirring up of spirits who are asleep. We have seen the evidence of that.

We *are* intercessors when we pray on behalf of our families and those in our families that are asleep spiritually. If we have been releasing Godly bonds for them, and it has awakened their spirits. This is the same principle.

What are earmarks of the loss of innocence in people?

The earmarks are in their DNA, the simple fact that we're born. That is the number one ear marker. *All* our innocence has been stolen in some way.

---

*The heart of the Father
is to continually be restoring
humanity back into Himself.*

The tools, this revelation, these are taking away the hindrances that have been upon the hearts and minds through the spirit of religion. These are effective. They are effective in intercessory work. They are effective when we pray for our family. Use these effectively. Remember the color of the bags is for our understanding of what we can capture or what we can release. It is just one of the tools.

Commission for the Pink Capture Bags[36]

We have seen two capture bags that are in time and out of time—purple and pink. As we are doing this work, we may see where pink is utilized.

I call my angels near, and I call Ezekiel, his commanders, and his ranks near.

I am requesting that you, in the name of Jesus, use the pink bags to capture and bring back from the very beginning—from the hand of the Father to now—the Innocence that has been stolen throughout the generations.

I repent on behalf of my generations for agreeing with the enemy that took away and stole the Innocence all the way back to the garden, even to the hand of the Father, and that corrupted my DNA and RNA.

I request that this be brought back to my realms for my spirit in the name of Jesus.

One someone has stood in the realms of Heaven and had their Innocence restored, they will be handed a garment—a garment of Innocence. Put it on, and speak to our soul, "Soul, do not be a gatekeeper. Accept this garment of Innocence. It has been given as a gift from the

---

[36] Feel free to adapt this to your situation.

Father. Body, accept this garment of Innocence as it begins to reconstruct my DNA and RNA, in Jesus' name."

We then decided to do the same for a friend we shall call Robin. Stephanie said,[37]

> *I call Robin's angels near to co-labor with Ezekiel, his commanders, and ranks with my angels, and commission you to go back in time and out of time on behalf of Robin, as we repent on behalf of the generations for partnering with and for being a part of the Innocence stolen that has affected the DNA and the RNA all the way back to the hand of the Father.*
>
> *I commission you to bring back the Innocence that has been stolen.*
>
> *I call Robin's spirit into heavenly realms to have the garment of Innocence placed upon her. I speak to Robin's spirit to teach the soul not to be a gatekeeper, to accept and receive this, and to bring this Innocence into her body, to change her DNA and RNA back to the Innocence that the Father designed in His original plan for us, in Jesus' name.*

Aren't we glad that Innocence can be brought back to the body? Many people will struggle with this concept because they have divulged themselves into false

---

[37] Feel free to adapt this to your situation.

understanding that the Father cannot restore innocence that has been stolen. This goes to that Scripture where they believe in godliness, but not the power of it."[38]

I was reminded of a testimony I heard of a woman who had been a prostitute. She got born again, and it was important to her to have her innocence restored. She just cried to the Lord for that. Sometime later, she ended up getting remarried and on her wedding night, her sheets were bloody. Her innocence had been restored.

We talked a few moments of how important this is for children whose innocence was stolen by others, for those who have been involved in sex trafficking or similar things. Having Innocence restored can go a long way to wholeness for them, and Heaven has obliged us with a simple way to see Innocence restored.

Malcolm reminded us that even though we do not have a full understanding of how this works, it is all done in the spirit realm.

Stephanie said, "I accept all that Heaven has. I was just trying to get clarification on how this was the only bag that was used as we step into Heaven."

Malcolm replied, "It's because of the purity there. That is where the innocence is put upon us, and it is brought into our realms."

---

[38] 2 Timothy 3:5

The Angel Purity

Innocence and the Angel Purity co-labor. Purity has longed with the heart of the Father regarding Innocence for people—Innocence and Purity. The completion of their work is that they are one.

As an act of faith, when I step into Heaven, and I ask for the Innocence to be brought back to me and I are robed with it; Purity's job, the work that she will do as I bring Innocence to my realms, to my spirit, soul, and body, is the knitting together of my being.

I commission you, Purity, to take my garment of Innocence that I have received in Heaven and to knit it to my soul and to my body, in Jesus' name.

These commissions are part of the redeeming because of how they release our angels to work.

I remarked about something I had learned from Joseph Sturgeon[39] that Purity had worked with Noah when it was said, *"He was made perfect in his generations."*[40] Purity worked with Noah and his DNA to remove the spots. Because he stepped into Heaven and received his innocence, and because he forgave his ancestors (Noah understood iniquity in the generations

---

[39] *Treasures of Darkness, Volume 2: Echoes of a Father* by Joseph Sturgeon, Feline Graphics (2016)

[40] Genesis 6:9

because the Lord had revealed that to him), he did what looked like courtroom work on behalf of his generations. This was part of the restoration of his innocence and the restoration of his DNA and RNA.

Moses, when he was on the mountain, and as he is coming down his face shone so brightly that they had to cover his face. The only reason it happened in the natural is because there was restoration to his soul and his body of the innocence that had been stolen, which in turn brought the knitting of that innocence to his soul and his body because of her work.

When there is innocence there is purity.

They all live in the same house together. They are one in that sense, because without corruption, when there's true Innocence the way the Father created us to be, there is purity.

Purity then showed how Eve, even though she was deceived and ate of the fruit, lost her purity. She still had Innocence, but Adam lost both at the same time when he ate of the fruit. In a sense, Innocence is something we wear. That is why it can be easily discarded when we sin, but it is also how it is corrupted in generations.

Capture Bag Commission[41]

Now that we have read about the various capture bags, I thought it would be appropriate to provide a template for commissioning our angels regarding the use of capture bags.

I call the angels assigned to me to come near.

Father, I request on behalf of these angels, all the different sizes, classifications, and colors of every capture bag needed to serve the Kingdom of Heaven and to serve your people in Jesus' name.

I commission the angels assigned to me to use every classification, size, and color of capturing bag needed; to go and capture the infiltrations; to use the different colors and classifications of the bags as needed from the smallest demon to the largest domain, in the name of Jesus; to use these capturing bags throughout my realms and those of my family.

I commission you to network and cooperate with Ezekiel, his commanders, and ranks and to work with the Bond Registry angels, in Jesus' name.

---

[41] Feel free to adapt this to your situation.

Chapter 19

Unweaving Domains

As Stephanie and I engaged this day, we were taken to a conference room. We sat at the conference table and on the table in the room was a map. It appeared that the entire table was a map. A man in white named Timothy[42] was also with us. We had met with him on a prior occasion. He informed us that he was from the Strategy Room. We could see what looked like stitching on the map that delineated one area from another like we see on a map showing the border of states or countries. The stitching was the border between domains. This lesson was to go along with the Lessons on Liening.

This type of domain is different than an internet domain. This is *like* a territory, but we must consider it a domain. The stitching that we saw was a weaving—an

---

[42] Timothy is a man in white who assisted us.

intertwining of domains which is a corruption upon the land and how we see territories. Territories can be in the natural, but they are in the spirit as well. In the supernatural, the wicked want territory. They despise losing territory so, we need to undo the weaving, so they lose more territory.

The strategies for undoing these things come from the Strategy Room. Angels can detect and see the domains, the stitching, and the weaving of the territories from the enemy. This is upon the territories of people's realms, their hearts, and their minds. The Lessons in Lienings will obstruct the enemy from the weaving as we walk in this prayer paradigm of the Courts of Heaven.

Our tutors, Malcolm and Timothy, were saying that this is the next part of learning about liening and capturing bags, because we must use the capturing bags in equipping our angels for capturing domains. This is part of that.

Remember we are a region. Our body, our soul, and our spirit are each a realm, Realms[43] comprise territories. Principalities are over regions and territories. That is what we have learned in the natural. Now we are learning that it is also spiritual within realms of a person. Let's undo the weaving by dealing with the

---

[43] Each part of our being is a realm. We are a spirit, with a soul that resides in a body. These realms have bridges one to another as well as gates through which information and other things pass.

parameters[44] that have resulted in the capture of a domain by the enemy.

With the map seen earlier the illustration we were given showed a land mass on the map. Then, we saw the stitching between the domains and that the enemy had control of this. He had weaved himself into another piece of territory, and that weaving together has created a bond, a stitching together. It is not like a tether or a soul tie. It is a weaving together. Remember what we learned about Lessons on Liening. *The same ease in the Court of Cancellations through this work will undo the weaving.*[45]

This was part of the same but was a clearer understanding. The weaving is a condition that has been placed upon the lien. We need to know what the condition was that permitted this and discovered it was bloodshed. The shedding of blood was the trade that allowed the principality to weave the territories together. This happened generationally.

In this scenario we were made to understand that it was the generational line that made the sacrifice upon the land that brought the principality into the generational line because of the parameters put upon the trust. It created a stitching between the generations. That is why it came down generation after generation after

---

[44] Parameters are essentially allegations placed against Godly trusts in our lives to neutralize the Godly trust and its benefits for us.

[45] This is explained more thoroughly in my book, *Dealing with Trusts & Consequential Liens in the Courts of Heaven*, LifeSpring Publishing (2022).

generation. That is how it had been able to do it in time and out of time.

How can a principality be able to follow a generational line? When the DNA is corrupted. The blood sacrifice allowed the condition for the principality to create the generational weaving from one generation to the next. The trade that was made allowed the principality to follow the generations down the line. It was time to do some unweaving.

We undo the weaving in the Court of Cancellations after the repentance work on behalf of the generations in the Court of Cancellations, as we cancel every covenant, oath, vow, bloodshed and the impacts and ramifications of them, and have the angels strike the parameters. We then commission the angels to use the capture bags in time and out of time. This will undo the weaving in the generations. It's an unstitching. It's an overturning. It's an undoing and the finished work [of Jesus] will be complete because the finished work is complete.

Undoing the Weaving

1. Access the Court of Cancellations
2. Repent for the generations opening the door and permitting the wickedness to continue
3. Cancel every covenant, oath, vow, bloodshed along with every impact and ramification of them
4. Have the angels strike the parameters

5. Commission the angels with capture bags in time and out of time

At times we will need what we needed to comprehend this information. Malcolm supplied us with a Garment of Ease. He said, "The ease of this flow will come to all that work in this."[46]

We were told the angels in the Strategy Room were excited that this information was being released. They were celebrating the fact that the angels are utilizing the strategies, and the capturing bags, and are co-laboring with us as we are doing this paradigm work with the Courts of Heaven and how much of an impact it is going to have upon lives of people.

> *Ezekiel, I commission you, your commanders, and your ranks to undo the weaving on behalf of LifeSpring International Ministries, Sandhills Ecclesia, CourtsNet, Heaven Down Business, and the other ministries, as well as for every employee and their families, in the name of Jesus.*
>
> *I request of the Father a Garment of Ease. I request that a Garment of Ease be given to every person on the ministry team, and those that have purchased the book, or attended one of our*

---

[46] If your soul is struggling at this moment, pause and ask Holy Spirit to grant a Garment of Ease to you.

conferences for this new revelation that Heaven has brought.

Ezekiel, we commission you to administer this Garment of Ease for this revelation on behalf of the Kingdom of Heaven, in Jesus' name.

Ezekiel then placed a Garment of Ease on both of us and we watched as he went to his commanders and ranks to begin instructing them about the Garments of Ease and the capturing bags he had in his hands. Stephanie was amazed at the vast number of ranks of angels gathered.

We thanked Malcolm and Timothy for their assistance. Timothy said, "I am leaving this map on this table because we will be seeing it again."

As we unweave domains, we are also unweaving the lingering spirits that have been assigned to your generations. *Much of what we have called familiar spirits are not demons, but lingering human spirits on assignment by demonic guards* and when we see them in family lines, again it is probably not a demon, but lingering spirits assigned to torment and afflict. With this work dealing with the principalities involved, freedom will come on a greater level.

———·———

Chapter 20

The Banners of the Lord

As we engaged Heaven at this time, the room was suddenly filled with Angels. Ezekiel appeared, so, prompted by Holy Spirit we began a commissioning in his behalf:

> *I commission you, Ezekiel, your commanders, and your ranks to break the standard of old to remove its powers, its frequencies, its hindrances, its telecommunications, and its systems.*
>
> *Do this by use of every capturing bag, in time, out of time, and in every dimension. Take it and destroy it, in the name of Jesus.*
>
> *Use the armaments of Heaven and the weaponry of Heaven. Use your good skill, in Jesus' name.*
>
> *I commission you to remove any old banners that you see and replace the old banner with the*

Banner of the Lord, to stake it, mark it, and highlight it, in Jesus' name!

Father, I also ask on all their behalf, angel food, angel bread, and angel elixir.[47]

The vision appeared like a movie being played as the lights in the room dimmed and a movie began playing on the screen that had appeared. Everyone in the room was watching a movie of some angelic activity. One could see a variety of landscapes. Some with cities and towns. One could see a mapping of people's minds. Scattered about the landscape, the angels were planting red flags (banners) where the territories had been reclaimed and restored. The flags were on tall poles so the enemy could see that this was territory that had been taken and given back to the Kingdom of Heaven, because of the blood, because of the commissioning, because of the co-laboring, and because of the obedience. The movie explained all this as the reason this movement is taking place.

As often happens, when Heaven uses a word, that word often has multiple meanings for what they want to teach us. The word was 'movement' and we could see the movement of when the earth moves under the force of an earthquake as it realigns itself and shifts. We also saw a movement, as in the Body of Christ, coming together and moving in unison. When they stake the banners in

---

[47] You are welcome to adapt this to your circumstances.

the ground, initially the ground is barren, and then, it becomes lush after the banner is staked in the ground. An innumerable number of angels was doing this work. We were invited by Malcolm to "taste and see that the Lord is good."[48]

We had been granted that vision because we had chosen the Kingdom of Heaven and the co-laboring—not only with angels but also the men and women in white and the other living creatures we were being introduced to. We chose the co-laboring. We chose the partnership. We chose the love of our Savior and of our Father. This is Kingdom dynamics.

Not only were we seeing the vision in relation to geographical land masses, but also people's minds, minds that were barren and ugly, like scorched earth but were becoming lush green with rich colors.

What is significant, is that we did not view it or see it as we would see the banners. It was like how they used to capture kingdoms and they would put the new flag up staking the ground as theirs. That was what this was—the capturing of dominions, capturing of domains, and the overturning of principalities. It is putting up the new flag.

The movie ended and they turned the lights back on in the room, then Wisdom came in and said, "I'm pleased with the revelation that's been revealed and is being

---

[48] Psalm 34:8

utilized because of the importance of it, because we are dealing with principalities."

She reiterated to us the importance of us utilizing her in every scenario and situation when it comes to that work. She gave Stephanie a big pearl much larger than one she had been given on a prior engagement. With that, Wisdom went and stood along the wall.

Jesus came into the room, and it became filled with love. He said,

---

The red flags were not for us to see. It was for the enemy to see that territory had been taken back.

Love enveloped the room because the people had been freed of the domination of the dominion. They could now begin to experience His love. Jesus explained that relational freedom would be found by people in this as the banners were being raised, and the flags were being turned back to Jesus, and as the territories were returned to Him when the stakes were placed in the ground.

The day prior, Stephanie and I had engaged Heaven and were taught about the red banners and the Banner of the Lord. This day, as we stepped in, we could see Ezekiel waving a red flag for the Conquering King—Jesus.

We were in a conference room and Ezekiel was pleased to have the red flag that he was waving.

Ezekiel explained what we were seeing. He said that many things were being accomplished in the spirit through the revelation and the co-laboring but there was much more to be done. This was Heaven's way of sharing that the Conquering King had conquered because *things had been conquered.*"

Many people live their lives with things going well, but for others it seems like things are not feeling very conquered. The demonstration from the earlier movie shows that there are specific things that the Conquering King has conquered based on the prayer paradigms used and the co-laboring with the angels that the things have been taking place. It is an assurance of the Conquering Kings work.

Ezekiel reiterated by placing a banner like a stake in what seemed to be the ground but instead was on a map of the brain. He stated that they were taking back fresh territory of mindsets.

As we watched the vision that unfolded, we saw lot of different angels, and they were conquering separate places in the brain. It was a demonstration of the cancellation of consequential liens upon people's lives that even caused a change their thinking. Their brain had appeared like scorched earth. Thought processes, synapses, intelligence, or even the perception of someone's intelligence within themselves are changed when that freedom occurs as it is redeemed by the Blood of the Lamb—redeemed by the Conquering King.

Angels have been waiting for these times, for this age of co-laboring. From the simplest commissioning to the greatest, it is their joy and honor to labor for the King.

I call the angels assigned to us to come near.[49]

Based on the knowledge that, because of Father's calling to the sons to act to forgive as John 20:23 instructs us and based on Romans 8:33 stating that God is the Judge who has issued HIS final verdict over them of not guilty, I commission the innumerable warring and capture angels who have been called for such a time as this.

I commission you to be released this minute, in time and out of time and in every dimension, using the full resources of Heaven, HIS Kingdom, HIS authority, to war on behalf of the peoples.

I commission you to bring about the swift changes meant for and on behalf of the land, this nation, the people, the minds, and the hearts of men.

I commission you to take the bounty that formerly belonged to the princes...to remove them and their ranks under them, to capture the dominion and the domain, the kingdom, the structures, the iron gates, and the foundations.

---

[49] You are welcome to adapt this to your situation.

I commission you to take the plunder that belongs to THE Kingdom of Heaven...and His sons. To take the broken ungodly standards of old, and to break them and burn them.

I commission you to place firmly the Banner of the Lord and then I request that ownership be given back to King Jesus.

This commission went to Ezekiel, his commanders, and his ranks to do that work.

We were charged to remind the people that are associated with LifeSpring International Ministries—those on Tuesday night, the Platinum Members—those that trade with LifeSpring, that because of that trade, those that trade with LifeSpring they have full utilization to have their angels link arms with Ezekiel's ranks and commanders. He said that the commissions had been great.

The people have been using these commissions to draw upon this knowledge and understanding and to use it to their advantage. It is for their advantage. It is a gift from the King. The utilization of angel armies is a gift. Angel armies are well-equipped to do this on behalf of the sons and they await with great anticipation every time we commission them. There is a joint co-laboring.

It seems a little bit one sided where we do the commissioning, and they do all the work and that is true. However, they enjoy the co-laboring, and they enjoy coming alongside and helping us to know how to commission them with what to say—it is a dual thing.

Understanding the Force of Co-Laboring

We next inquired what commissioning they needed, and he began to describe the functions of his various commanders and ranks. Ezekiel began showing us that some of the commanders, their specific job is undoing the weaving, for other commanders, their specific jobs were the use of capture bags. Some were going to release other angels. There were specific jobs for each of the commanders.

We understood that concept, but Ezekiel wanted us to understand the force behind this concept of co-laboring with angels, that it presented a force to be reckoned with that has been laid upon the foundations of LifeSpring because of the understanding of co-laboring. He reminded us of a time when we saw the number of angels grow in number. He said that they continue to do that.

> *Ezekiel, I commission you, your commanders, and ranks to the undoing of territories and joined land masses and domains, as necessary.*
>
> *I request of the Father capture bags of every size and color and purpose to be released to them.*
>
> *I commission you for the full use of these capture bags based upon their purpose.*

I release you to do that.

I commission you for releasing understanding to the people that are joined with us in the ministry.

I commission you to those who are to fund the various aspects of the ministry and to bring favor for those working on behalf of the ministry.

Father, I am requesting on their behalf golden lassos.

I commission you, Ezekiel, to use the golden lassos and take what would have been the frequencies of a storm and collapse them right before our feet.

I commission the angels that are specified to the unweaving to undo the weaving, in the mighty name of Jesus.

I ask for more encampments on behalf of Ezekiel. I thank You, Father. Thank You for the growth. It is a gift from You, Father. I thank You for that.

I commission you, Ezekiel, to take the Banner of the Lord and the poles and stake it in the ground with the red flag on behalf of the ministry and all aspects of it, in Jesus' name.

I commission you to collapse every storm, use fog dispeller as necessary, and every weaponry at your disposal on behalf of the ministry, those who *are part of the team, and those connected to the ministry in any fashion, in Jesus' name.*

The Personal Guarantee

Lydia, Malcolm, George,[50] and Wisdom were in the room and George came forth holding a piece of paper in his hand—a document that he had signed. He explained the paper to us, "It is a Personal Guarantee of the Father for funds for the processes, plans, and purposes of Heaven having the backing of a personal guarantee by the Father of <u>*everything*</u> being fully funded. He wanted this to be on record for all."

We thanked George and took the copy he gave us, as he kept a copy to put on file for us.

He reminded us that every assignment from Heaven is fully funded.

Wisdom at the Table

Wisdom then took a seat at the table. Normally she stood. She began showing how Wisdom grows within the hearts of men as we utilize her.

---

[50] George a man in white who is the Chief Financial Officer for the ministry.

There is a strength and a literal growth within the person's spirit and soul every time we call upon her and invoke her in a situation. Wisdom grows inside our realms, inside of our hearts, and our minds. As we gain more and more understanding from her, relationship builds, and relationship grows, and we always have a seat at the table with her.

Wisdom showed us that it was like the Father has taken a piece of Himself—a piece out of Himself, and that is who Wisdom is. Of course, we know that Wisdom is one of the Seven Spirits of God. She wanted the people to see this as a picture—to understand that she is a true entity within the deity—that she can grow and build inside of each person that invokes her, calls upon her, walks with her, holds her hand, or utilizes her in every situation. It creates an internal strength inside us, it becomes like steel inside of us—unwavering, unmoved. Full understanding and knowledge come with that growth. It is like a steely position within somebody. It is as iron inside of someone. It is incredibly strong inside a person and so it is as we walk with each of the Seven Spirits of God—Wisdom, Understanding, Knowledge, Counsel, Understanding, Might, and the Fear of the Lord.

———·———

Chapter 21

Overcoming the Familial Spirit

We have noticed an uptick in the workings of the entity referred to as the familiar spirit recently. This may be related to the season we are in (which is quite likely) or just simply an uptick in a particular kind of assault.

A familiar spirit is one who is familiar with us. A familial spirit is one (or more) attached to a bloodline that impacts every generation of that bloodline.

A familiar spirit was what the medium and Endor was expecting when she sought to summon Samuel on behalf of Saul. She did not get what she was expecting but had enough understanding that a Man in White stood before her—a son of God—a *benai elohim*.

Familiar (and familial) spirits know our comings and goings, and they know well our triggers. They know our patterns, and they know how to get us to react in certain situations. They will orchestrate situations to bring about defeat, despair, hopelessness, and a sense of surrender to whatever their voice is saying at the time. They follow patterns. They desire to get us to possess a thought as our own thought when it is contrary to who we are. They will motivate us to act contrary to what we know is Heaven's best for us and get us self-focused. The self-focusing is a clue to the fact that they are at work.

Familial spirits are particularly familiar with our family and know the strengths and weaknesses of it.

Neither familiar or familial spirits are terribly bright and therefore do not have a large bag of tricks from which to pull from. Their operations are rather simple and predictable once we discern the patterns. The pattern for one person will likely be the same pattern used for another person and if a familial spirit will know the generational tendencies.

Also, we are probably not dealing with a demonic entity but rather a lingering spirit on assignment. That would easily explain their familiarity to us and our family—how we think, act, react, etc.

We heard Heaven say,

> *"In this season we will see an uptick in the operation of the familiar spirit."*

The familiar spirit wants us to focus on ourselves and our failures rather than on the Risen King who lives inside us. They will seek to say we are not good enough and we don't do well enough to do the things we do. They want to pull us down.

> *Just as the mark of a religious spirit is a sense of powerlessness, the mark of a familiar spirit is a sense of failure.*

The sense of failure is accusation driven and will be incessant unless we take a firm stand, deal with the accusations, and dismantle them, and repossess the mind of Christ that the familiar spirit has sought to take from us.

> *We are a possessor of the mind of Christ.*

His way of thinking is contrary to our old way of thinking when we were bound in religion and tradition. The new way of thinking requires a constant embrace of the truth the Father says about us.

The Scripture we know of from Paul's writing in Philippians will help us.

Philippians 4:4-9:

⁴ Rejoice in the Lord always. Again, I will say, rejoice! ⁵ Let your gentleness (your peace-driven way of life) be known to all men. The Lord is at hand. ⁶ Be anxious for nothing, but in everything by prayer and supplication, with thanksgiving, let your requests be made known to God; ⁷ and the peace of God, which surpasses all understanding, will guard your hearts and minds through Christ Jesus.

⁸ Finally, brethren, whatever things are true, whatever things are noble, whatever things are just, whatever things are pure, whatever things are lovely, whatever things are of good report, if there is any virtue and if there is anything praiseworthy—meditate on these things.

⁹ The things which you learned and received and heard and saw in me, these do, and the God of peace will be with you.

Now read this same passage from The Mirror[51]:

⁴ Joy is not a luxury option; joy is your constant! Your union in the Lord is your permanent source of delight; so, I might as well say it again, rejoice in the Lord always! ⁵ Show perfect courtesy towards all people! The Lord is not nearer to some than what He is to others! ⁶ Let no anxiety about anything ¹distract you! Rather translate moments into prayerful worship, and soak your requests in gratitude before God! ⁷ And in this place of worship and gratitude you will witness how the peace of God within you echoes the awareness of

---

[51] du Toit, Francois. *Mirror Study Bible* (p. 731). Kindle Edition.

your oneness in Christ Jesus beyond the reach of any thought that could possibly unsettle you. Just like the ¹sentry guard secures a city, watching out in advance for the first signs of any possible threat, your hearts deepest feelings and the tranquility of your thoughts are fully guarded there. (This peace is not measured by external circumstances; it is residing deeply in the innermost parts of your being. We are not talking about a fragile sense of peace that can easily be disturbed; one that we must fabricate ourselves; this is God's peace; the peace that God himself enjoys!)

⁸ *Now let this be your conclusive reasoning:*

- *Consider that which is true about everyone as evidenced in Christ.*

- *Live overwhelmed by God's opinion of you!*

- *Acquaint yourselves with the revelation of righteousness.*

- *Realize God's likeness in you.*

- *Make it your business to declare mankind's redeemed innocence.*

- *Think friendship.*

- *Discover how famous everyone is in the light of the gospel; mankind is in God's limelight!*

- *Ponder how elevated you are in Christ.*

- *Study stories that celebrate life. (See Col 3:3, "Engage your thoughts with throne room realities where we are co-seated together with Christ!"[52]*

Our enemy says that if he can steal our joy, he can keep our goods! Don't let him steal your joy by falling into his trap.

Anxiety is proof we have dropped our guard.

We have allowed joy to be removed from the equation that is our life because an atmosphere of anxiety invites defeat. Anxiety is undefined fear, and we are not to cooperate with fear on any level at any time in any fashion. Anxiety will paralyze faith and cause a cessation of victory in our realms. Anxiety comes from the soul realm, will manifest in the body realm, and will override the spirit realm of a person. Remember that Isaiah 26:3 says,

---

[52] du Toit, Francois. *Mirror Study Bible* (p. 730-731). Kindle Edition.

You will keep him in perfect peace, whose mind is stayed on You, because he trusts in You.

Perfected peace is a result of focus
on the Father's thoughts of us.

In the Mirror translation of Philippians 4 quoted earlier, verse 8 instructs us to live overwhelmed by God's opinion of us. We do this by acquainting ourselves more fully of the revelation of righteousness—which is to realize God's likeness in us.

The writer says to make it our business to declare mankind's redeemed innocence. Declare that to ourselves.

The voice of the familiar spirit
must be identified and then
made to surrender to the voice
of the redeemed son.

Paul said to think friendship—we are in partnership with the Father and *are automatically fulfilling His will just by being us.* We don't have to find God's will; we are already IN God's will—we ARE God's will. Wherever we find ourselves, we find ourselves in God and He in us.

Jesus said,

The Kingdom of God is within you. (Luke 17:21)

It is not in a faraway elusive place. The realm of God and His dominion is closer than we have been made to believe. By surrendering the inferior understanding, we surrender the strength of that understanding. The writer is giving us a step-by-step approach to full mind renewal.

The thoughts of the familiar spirit are contrary thoughts to the thoughts of the redeemed son.

It matters not what we have done in our past or any past failures as we would define them. The fact that we are considering these truths will help us unveil the Christ in us. Where we allow our thoughts to take us is where we will remain.

We are famously fashioned in the likeness of God! We are NOT fashioned in the likeness of a fallen creature. The thoughts of fallenness do not derive from the presence of God. They are the outworking of religion, and the horrendous concepts that fallenness produces in we are designed to keep us from becoming the light we are. We are to shine—famously, and we do as we walk in the peace provided by our Father. (Isaiah 60:1)

A familiar spirit will seek to drive us from the peace that is our possession.

When we sense our peace being absent from us, take note of where our mind has gone. Corral the thoughts that have made no room for the perfect and perfected peace of God in our life. Ponder how elevated we are in Jesus. We are taken to a whole new place that we could not have taken ourselves to. We are instructed to engage our thoughts in heavenly realities. Ponder what God thinks of us—not on our perceived defeats and failures.

Are we doing everything perfectly at this point in our life? Of course not.

> *We are learning and relearning the Father's ways of thinking.*

The Father sees us as righteous because Jesus made that provision for us on the cross. He sealed it by the utter defeat of sin and its power over our life via the resurrection. Righteousness is two parties finding likeness in each other where there is no sense of inferiority, suspicion, blame, regret, or pressure to perform. All these thoughts are contrary to thinking on things of good report. They are all but a good report.

> *A familiar spirit rejoices in our defeat.*

He will make us feel as if what we are doing is not good enough to please the Father, and instead of getting better at what we are doing for the Father, he invites us to completely give up on what we are doing and concede surrender.

He will cause us to be suspicious and begin comparing ourselves to another who is doing things "better" than us in an area. At that point, he does not magnify the other person's struggles. He magnifies our inferiority in relation to what they do.

He will cause us to blame ourselves, our circumstances, our position in life, our neighborhood, the darkness over our city... anything but the true enemy, which is Satan. He is *always* deflecting blame.

The familiar spirit drives us to regret

...regret that we can't see as well as so and so, or hear as well as that other person, or know what Dr. Ron, or Stephanie know. Of course, we don't! That is their journey, not our journey!

The Father is not measuring one's journey to another's!

For us, He is only focused on our journey. He is working to see that all that is needed for the successful completion of our journey is that we remain *on* that journey.

The Blame Game

If the familiar spirit is unable to stop us with feelings of inferiority, or suspicion, or getting us to play the blame game, he will proceed to get us to move from where we are to a place of regret. The place of regret is a lonely place, and we have no business living in it.

The next step in the progression of defeat and surrender to the familiar spirit is the place of "**pressure to perform.**" We are always measuring what we do against an imaginary checklist of duties to perform.

- Did we pray long enough this morning?
- Did we read the Bible like we committed to at the beginning of the year?
- Did we go through all our rituals of prayer this morning?
- Are we praying constantly?

The list can be endless. The Father is not nearly as concerned about our lists as we are. He wants *us*.

---

*The more we are enveloped in Him
the more He is enveloped in us.*

The gospel is the revelation of the righteousness of God; it declares how God succeeded to put mankind right with Him. It is about what God did right, not what Adam did wrong...nor about what WE have done wrong.

---

*Evil spirits will always focus on real,
perceived, or imagined failures.*

They want us to focus on our prior estate and not on what Father has been doing successfully in our life.

Are we stronger in our walk today than we were 3 months ago? If we can say, "yes," then we have made progress.

In this chapter, wherever I have spoken of a familiar spirit, similar traits are those of the familial spirit. We can basically use the phrases interchangeably knowing that a familial spirit specializes in a family line.

Dealing with a Familiar/Familial Spirit

Recognizing who we are dealing with is simple:

- Ask the question of Heaven, "Am I dealing with a familiar spirit?" If the answer is yes,
- Then ask, "Who sent you?" You are looking for the boss.
- Ask Holy Spirit to help us identify who the boss is, then deal with it by repentance. Often, we have fallen into traps that we have learned from our family, our friends, co-workers, workplace, or church.
- Once we have discovered the boss, ask "Are you operating through a lingering human spirit? (If the answer is yes, instruct them to come forth so we can minister to them.)
- Repent for cooperation on any level that gave access to these patterns in our life.
- Repent for allowing it entrance in our life and giving it more than two seconds of our thoughts to begin to destroy things in our life.
- Once the repentance is complete, simply speak to boss/principality declaring to it that his assignment is over, and he must go.

- Ask angels to ensure that he is removed from the scene.
- Then address the demonic guards/familiar spirits informing them that their assignment is over and request angels to take them to the feet of Jesus. (They are not too thrilled to be in His presence.)
- If a lingering spirit is involved, minister to them with respect and instruct them to request mercy of the Father when they stand before Him.
- Open the silver channel and have angels assist their transition.
- Once the lingering spirit has transitioned, close the silver channel.
- Request angels to cleanse all our realms of all spiritual debris left by the demons or the lingering spirits.
- Then, step into freedom from the place of regret or inferiority, or wherever we have been standing. Each of these words: inferiority, suspicion, blame, regret, or pressure to perform, is a place we step into.
- See it as a place that we are choosing to move out of.
  - We will no longer live in Inferiority.
  - We will no longer live in Suspicion.
  - We will no longer live in Blame, Regret, or Pressure to Perform.
  - We are moving out! **It is moving day!**

During this season we will have to monitor our thoughts diligently, continuously capturing thoughts of ill toward others, of defeat, despair, or other thoughts not borne of Holy Spirit or of Heaven in our life. Elevate our thoughts to new places this season. Just as the angels told the shepherds that they brought good news that would cause great joy in the coming of a Savior, so the Savior has come to us, to our life, to our thoughts. Rejoice!

Now to identify precisely what we are dealing with, we can use bi-lateral questions or check in the Guest Registry, then follow the procedure for releasing lingering human spirits—whether familiar or familial in nature. If using the Guest Registry, do a sort by familiar or familial to determine which we are dealing with, then conduct a sort within that by source of the familiar or familial spirit—whether an LHS or demon. We have already been instructed in what to do, so handle it.

Remember, Jesus indicated that a spirit that had gone out of a person would migrate back toward their family with whom they are most familiar. It would provide a perfect opportunity for the enemy to hijack them and become their demonic guard to harass someone. Just go through the process for freedom and enjoy the joy that comes with freedom!

Chapter 22

Migrating LHS's

& Double Dipping

In recent dealings with clients, we have noticed a new phenomenon—that of LHS's the seem to migrate from person to person, particularly those of the same household or those with close soul ties to one another.

Person to Person Migration

In one case, the LHS was moving from Mom to Dad to the son. When checking the registry of the Mom, the LHS was listed. The advocates in that session simply requested angels keep him where he could be seen. That is when they found this LHS had been moving from person to person to person creating havoc in the realms of each and keeping things stirred up between them. Fortunately, the team was able to aid in the transition of the LHS after dealing with the demonic guard and the boss.

In another case a couple who had once been engaged, but never married yet remained close friends were another example of what I refer to as migrating LHS's. These individuals were constantly alternating weird sicknesses. One would be sick, while the other was recovering from being sick. Then they would get sick from something peculiar and the other would spend a few days in recovery from the most recent malady. The obvious solution—deal with the LHS and close the doors to future activity for both so, they can begin the journey of healing.

If we are ministering to someone and we see a pattern of alternating issues between persons that would have strong soul ties one to another, we may want to inquire if we are looking at a migrating LHS situation and deal with it accordingly.

Moving from Body Part to Body Part

Another manifestation of a migrating lingering spirit is one that moves from one body part to another, sometimes in a circle. They might afflict the right knee one day, the left ankle the next. In the process of afflicting us they are also letting us know that we have someone to deal with to usher them home.

Double-Dipping

Our adversary is an opportunist. However, he does not get the last word. Recently, Stephanie had a revelation arising from a question.

Stephanie explained:

I received this download that when a person dies, if they already had consequential liens and a principality attached to their life from the generations, that they were restricted, either by their belief that they could not transition into Heaven, or were scared to, or the principality hindered their transition.

What if the princes and the demons, because of the consequential liens and having princes lording over those already established liens, what if they continue the process after the person is dead? What if they then use that against the lingering human spirit (LHS) because the LHS still has a prince attached to their life? That's the one that we deal with, they are the boss in the end. It is like Satan is double dipping. He's keeping them from their access to Heaven, which is their inheritance, right? That consequential lien has kept them from realizing that they can step into Heaven. Then, he uses that prince and those demonic guards to torment the person. He is double dipping! That's a taxation. Isn't it? Let's go get everything back that we are owed!

I suggested we find out what Malcolm had to say about that thought, so we engaged Heaven shortly afterward and met with Malcolm. We queried about whether when a person passes away and they become a lingering spirit, if that person had a principality via a consequential lien or ungodly trust—can any of that keep a person from entering Heaven?

When a person at their death bed as soon as they slip out of their body the portal (silver channel) is in front of them. They will see angels and possibly also see demons. The reality is, when a person passes away, they have full knowledge of all things spiritual including entities. The veil has been removed. In the moment passing they are given that choice.

Malcolm asked us, "Do we really think the enemy stops his lies at the point of death? What is done from his kingdom it's not just to hurt the sons, it is to hurt the Father."

Satan *hates* the Father. The enemy knows there is restoration in this work! Satan's goal is to keep people from the Kingdom of Heaven as long as possible. The visual Stephanie had was that of a person standing there after death in what we would think of as outer space. It is the space between us (while alive)—that other side of the veil. They may see angels or demons, or other entities. When the person that died stepped out of their body, and if they have had a consequential lien or an ungodly trust put upon their trust, which is their inheritance—a prince may also be standing in that place saying they have no access. He reminds them of all their generations have done. He scares them into believing that they do not have access to their trust (inheritance) and that IF they do go in through the portal to Heaven, that there's only judgment awaiting them! Satan is just using people and LHS's to hurt the Father over and over and over.

If I'm the one that is just standing there, I see what is considered light and what is considered darkness on the other side of this veil. Can we imagine stepping out of our body and there's a big principality standing there like, 'Oh, no...we don't have a way in there.' Then we have an angel saying, "Come on, it's time, come on with me." Or we have a prince and all that is demonic saying, 'Oh, no! You have been way too bad. You're going to be judged!"

I replied, "They don't even have to see a prince for that, just a little peon demon."

All this time we have been dealing with the "boss" and the demonic guards. We have been dealing with the principality and the demons attached to some LHS's all along. If, when they were living, an ungodly trust was placed upon their trust in the Father—which involves the absolute walking in and stepping into our inheritance when we are alive *AND* when we die. That's why the Father is saying to us who are alive on the earth, that when we say about Him, 'I am the way the truth and the life,'[53] the Father has truly provided this way for those

---

[53] John 14:6

who believed in life after death, that felt they didn't deserve to step in, or that they were still in bondage and couldn't step over. The Father is saying, 'No, I am the way.' The enemy knew that there is a way and that the people of light—us, were going come into this concept and understanding of LHS work and provide help, provide with the co-laboring, and open the portal for them to go through! That's why (Satan) did not want the church to know about this—ever!"

There are people that are going to die, that aren't going to make the choice to come on into Heaven because they still are living under that demon or that prince that is lying to them at the point of their death, but God is saying 'I'm still providing away and I'm doing it through my sons that are living.'

John 20:23[54] is one of the most helpful Scriptures we can use to help LHS's, but another is found in Hebrews 9:27-28,

> *[27] And as it is appointed for men to die once, but after this the judgment (justice), [28] so Christ was offered once to bear the sins of many. To those who eagerly wait for Him He will appear a second time, apart from sin, for salvation.*

The Father is all about mercy and over judgment! Their justice *is* mercy. Since the Father handed over to

---

[54] John 20:23 "If you forgive the sins of any, they are forgiven them; if you retain the sins of any, they are retained."

Jesus[55] all judgment and sin, which was judged at the crucifixion, there's no more judgment for their sin.

> *Most assuredly, I say to you, he who hears My word and believes in Him who sent Me has everlasting life, and shall not come into judgment, but has passed from death into life. (John 5:24)*

At the cross every bit of judgment and accusations were on Him in that moment. There is no more judgment upon any of us. If people could grasp the principle that Satan hates the Father more than he hates them, they will realize he is just *using them to get to the Father*—to hurt Him, to get back at Him. The Father has provided a way above all ways and a means above all means. He's using His children of light to bring in those that walk in darkness into the reality that they have an inheritance."

It is the will of Father for those we have called LHS's to be recognized as persons, lingering human persons. They are 'persons'—persons that are still lingering.

Satan knew that God was going to still provide a way, and Satan has just been lying to us and lying to us some more. He has been taxing us. We know about taxations and how to cancel those because we know how to stop the taxation in our own lives.

We wanted to know if there is a taxation upon on our life is that why the enemy can put a lingering human

---

[55] John 5:22 "For the Father judges no one, but has committed all judgment to the Son."

spirit on us that has a demonic guard and a prince. Somebody must carry out the taxation. The question is, "Is it in the guest registry, and can we sort by taxations?"

When we ask Heaven, and they will reveal. We can ask if there is a taxation and if we close that taxation in our life it is going to prevent LHS's from coming at us that have been sent to us with a prince—one that has a boss and guards, because if we close the taxation route, we close the way.

———·———

Chapter 23

Speaking from the Grave

(A Testimony from Stephanie Shearin)

In my recent session, the Senior Advocate, and the Junior Advocate who were with me both saw and heard the same thing but used different words. It was discovered that an LHS was speaking who had been a 33rd Degree Mason. The difference in this setting was he was ruling over my generations *from the grave.*

I saw him in his coffin spouting orders. I commissioned the angels to put holy dirt on top of his grave and flood the coffin with Living Water and the blood of Jesus. Then, I saw him try to speak and his words only reverberated in the coffin, and it frightened him.

Joyce had the angels bring him from the coffin and had his voice sealed shut so he could not speak unless permitted. He had been able to communicate with his bloodline through what appeared to be soul ties or tethers.

Initially he was prideful and arrogant and happy with the pact he had made to be able to rule from the grave and basically not be sensed as an LHS.

Joyce took charge of the setting and began to pray:

> *Speaking to the man, she said, "Your voice is not worthy to be heard. There is a voice that is above all that we do listen to and it's the name of Jesus Christ. We call you to repent and bow your knees. We call you to turn off every sprinkling of every directive, fear tactic, assassination attempts, mischaracterization of justice, demonic intrusions, and calling of shots from the grave.*
>
> *We call you to repent and receive the Living Lord. Repent of your evil deeds, repent of the freemasonry, repent of every order & rite, benefit, regalia, and pomp and splendor, and of all the accolades you received. Repent of the hat you were given (that you took) as a chancellor. Repent. Hear my voice and receive the Voice of the Lord.*

Joyce then said, "In the name of Jesus, we cut every silver cord and voice and multiplicity of voices speaking through us. Today, the chord is cut, and we can no longer reveal ourselves or infuse ourselves or emanate in Stephanie's realms."

Joyce saw that the grave was then empty. She continued:

What you are using to speak (silver cords) you will no longer infuse yourself to emanate in her realms.

Joyce continued,

Angels, take him to the feet of Jesus. We ask the angels to take all voices from his voice, we ask that the ley-lines to be crumpled and destroyed. Remove all refuse and all evil frequencies. We cut the silver chord to others who were taking orders from him. All influence from his voice is cut in the name of Jesus!

Joyce described what she saw next and said,

The grave was emptied and the man, standing before the Lord. His hat was off, and his head was hanging in shame and his knees were wobbling.

[Stephanie testified that she could feel a tangible shift in her being since that LHS was dealt with. She has experienced new freedom and new clarity for which we praise the Father for.]

———·———

Chapter 24

Testimony of Freedom

(A Testimony from Linda Griebel)

About 5 years ago, I was biking a couple hours a day, several days a week. It became increasingly more difficult for me to raise my leg to get on and off my bike. I had no other issues. I backed off of biking, thinking my bike seat was the issue. Then, I noticed pain from my groin to my knee. I saw a doctor. My X-rays revealed my hips were out of alignment. My blood work was fine. Once again, I thought my bike seat was the culprit. My doctor referred me to physical therapy for six months. No improvement, even with exercise and traction. I received adjustment from a chiropractor three times a week for a year, with no improvement. In fact, I was getting worse. I called myself healed and declared healing scriptures over myself—I was just not seeing the improvement I expected.

I attended several healing services. I have been prayed over by Billy Burke, Tony Kemp, Keith Moore and several other people. When I was prayed for, it would be better for a while, but it did not last.

It was not consistently in the same place, it moved around. Sometimes I could walk just fine. Other times, I limped. At times, I could walk upstairs, others I could not. I would get a tingling sensation in my upper back on the right side where the rhomboids muscles are. The muscles there were tight.

I went fully on the Gerson Therapy diet protocol for people who are terminal. Thirteen glasses of juice a day, no meat, whole organic foods, and coffee enemas. I eat healthy, so this was not that difficult for me. I felt great, but it did not correct the problem.

I am familiar with Dr. Caroline Leaf and Dr. Henry Wright's training. I went through all 22 videos of Dr. Michelle Strydom's teaching from her book, *No Disease is Incurable*. My symptoms were very similar to rheumatoid arthritis.

Then, I reached out to Arthur Burke with Sapphire Leadership Group. Arthur asked if I had considered AHS's, Alien Human Spirits. I had not even heard of such a thing. I downloaded the teaching on AHS's from Sapphire Leadership Group's website. I found a book by Dr. Ron Horner, *Lingering Human Spirits*. I also purchased other books by Dr. Ron Horner on operating in the Courts of Heaven. I even completed a couple of online courses on their CourtsNet.com website.

I felt led to contact Dr. Ron Horner and to schedule a personal advocacy session with the COH ministry team. My first appointment was on Wednesday, April 20, 2022.

I was amazed at what was revealed in that session. I did have some lingering human spirits—seventeen were attached to me. One of these spirits was my father, Howard. With him were sixteen other spirits. There were two demonic guards: the spirit of death and the spirit of bitterness. I did not have a good understanding of this yet, but I knew more would be revealed to me by the Holy Spirit as I hungered for answers.

For some reason, my father could not go on without these other men's spirits. Once we had gone to the Courts of Heaven, these spirits were able to leave and go through the silver channel. A few days after my session, I spoke with my older sister. She told me that while our father was in the army during World War II, he had gotten very sick, which prevented him from being sent out on a mission with the sixteen other men in his squad. They were all killed on that mission.

Another interesting revelation was how the number 7 was significant in our generation line. My father died in October 2000. My mother died in October 2007. My younger sister died close to the same day in 2014. My father was 77 when he died. In the Courts of Heaven, the advocates and I dealt with curses over my generational line.

After my session, I began to have greater mobility and I was not so hungry all the time. Prior to this, I had a ravenous appetite (not unlike soldiers). It has been two months since my session, I have lost 17 pounds, and I am able to walk up and down stairs. I sleep without pain in my hips and back. I am getting stronger and gaining flexibility. I can tie my own shoes now, and I can carry my new grand babies without discomfort.

I had my thyroid tested regularly for the past 20 years. I was certain my increased appetite and the difficulty managing my weight was due to a thyroid issue. I took a neuro-transmitter prescription for over 20 years. I no longer feel the need to do so. I am not hungry all the time. Now when I eat, I can eat a normal amount and feel satisfied.

I have even dealt with a few more lingering human spirits by following the protocol in Dr. Ron Horner's book. I am very grateful for this ministry and will continue to train on the Courts Heaven. I have shared this information with several people that are suffering from similar symptoms. I pray they will receive freedom from the torment they may have endured for so long.

———·———

Chapter 25

Conclusion

We have discovered insights to assist us in ministering to the persons who have yet to transition into Heaven. We have discussed some of the reasons and even been saddened to understand that false or erroneous teachings have been responsible for many LHS's being unable or unwilling to transition simply because of some stupid belief system they embraced. That does not make the person stupid, it simply unveils the stupidity of some of our religious teachings. The truth will set us free, but lies will put us in bondage—lies that even impact us after death.

Thankfully, Heaven has been awakening us to things outside our religious boxes. These concepts are available to those willing to think a little differently and respond to the direction of Holy Spirit.

Prior to releasing the first volume of this series we heard many concerns that this would not be accepted by the Body of Christ at large. However, we have found many that this message and understanding resonate with. They can embrace that this is the heart of the Father to have ALL come to repentance,[56] just as Peter declared in his letters. The Father is not trying to fill up hell, he wants to fill up Heaven.

The more this work is accomplished the greater the peace will reign in our environments—our homes, businesses, churches, cities, states, and nations. This is a worldwide redemptive work.

Heaven has explained to us how helping lingering human persons to transition to their destiny in Heaven is a redemptive work on behalf of the Kingdom. Now that we have read these additional insights, may we be used to help thousands transition to their eternal destiny and create a hardship for the realms of darkness—all because Jesus reigns!

---

[56] 2 Peter 3:9

Appendix

Frequently Asked Questions

Why should I become a Christian now if I have the option of going to Heaven anyway by just asking for God's mercy?

We can find no definitive pattern for why (or whether) a human spirit enters directly into Heaven or hell or lingers for a time. If we take what has been discussed in this book and say to ourselves, "I don't have to serve God now, I can wait and get another chance even after I die." This would be a risk I would not recommend to anyone. Serve God with all our heart now!

Why do we use the term Lingering Human Spirit instead of Alien Human Spirit like some others do?

Personally, I feel that the term Lingering Human Spirit (LHS) more accurately captures the concept particularly considering the Scriptures in Matthew 12:43 and Luke 11:24-25. Additionally, all the press about aliens may confuse the issue. The terminology is secondary in my opinion.

What is purgatory?

According to the Catholic.com website:

"The Catechism of the Catholic Church defines purgatory as a 'purification, to achieve the holiness necessary to enter the joy of heaven,' which is experienced by those 'who die in God's grace and friendship, but still imperfectly purified' (CCC 1030). It notes that 'this final purification of the elect . . . is entirely different from the punishment of the damned.' (CCC 1031)." (Purgatory Tract, 2019)

Isn't this necromancy?

According to the Merriam-Webster Dictionary, necromancy, in short was the conjuration of the dead. The full definition is:

Conjuration of the spirits of the dead for purposes of magically revealing the future or influencing the course of events.[57]

The Biblical story to which most people allude is when King Saul sought out a medium to conjure up Samuel. Unfortunately, our translation of the story is rather weak and gives us a wrong understanding.

> *[7] Then Saul said to his servants, 'Find me a woman who is a medium, that I may go to her and inquire of her.' And his servants said to him, 'In fact, there is a woman who is a medium at En Dor.' [8] So Saul disguised himself and put on other clothes, and he went, and two men with him; and they came to the woman by night. And he said, 'Please conduct a séance for me, and bring up for me the one I shall name to you.' [9] Then the woman said to him, 'Look, you know what Saul has done, how he has cut off the mediums and the spiritists from the land. Why then do you lay a snare for my life, to cause me to die?' [10] And Saul swore to her by the LORD, saying, 'As the LORD lives, no punishment shall come upon you for this thing.' [11] Then the woman said, 'Whom shall I bring up for you?' And he said, 'Bring up Samuel for me.'*

---

[57] "Necromancy." *The Merriam-Webster.com Dictionary*, Merriam-Webster Inc., https://www.merriam-webster.com/dictionary/necromancy. Accessed 29 November 2019.

> *¹² When the woman saw Samuel, she cried out with a loud voice. And the woman spoke to Saul, saying, 'Why have you deceived me? For you are Saul!' ¹³ And the king said to her, 'Do not be afraid. What did you see?' And the woman said to Saul, 'I saw a spirit ascending out of the earth.' ¹⁴ So he said to her, 'What is his form?' And she said, 'An old man is coming up, and he is covered with a mantle.' And Saul perceived that it was Samuel, and he stooped with his face to the ground and bowed down. ¹⁵ Now Samuel said to Saul, 'Why have you disturbed me by bringing me up?' And Saul answered, 'I am deeply distressed; for the Philistines make war against me, and God has departed from me and does not answer me anymore, neither by prophets nor by dreams. Therefore, I have called you, that you may reveal to me what I should do.' (1 Samuel 28:7-15) (Emphasis mine)*

The medium was accustomed to working with a familiar spirit who would mimic the words and behavior of the person being sought by the conjuring. In this case she was taken aback (see v. 12) by what occurred. She declares to Saul that she had seen a spirit which implies to us (based on our old paradigms) that it was demon. The verse would be better translated "I saw an elohim ascending from the wilderness." An elohim is typically understood as "son of God" or "a son of God." She went on to describe what she was seeing, and Saul perceived it was Samuel (v.14). At that point, Saul begins to speak to Samuel who reiterates that the Lord had stripped the kingdom from Saul and had given it to David, his rival. We often have trouble with this passage and lump it together with the directives against conjuring up spirits for the purpose of knowing or altering the future. Jesus, on the Mount of Transfiguration spoke with Elijah and Moses.

In Matthew, He spoke to the crowd asking about the resurrection and tells them:

> *"'I AM the God of Abraham, the God of Isaac, and the God of Jacob'? God is not the God of the dead, but of the living." (Matthew 22:32)*

However, at the time Jesus spoke to the crowd, the bodies of Abraham, Isaac, and Jacob had been dead for centuries. Maybe our view of the dead needs to be adjusted to understand that they still live—just in another realm.

As we are not seeking to gain insight into the future or to alter the whole scheme of things on the earth, we are not engaging in necromancy. If that were so, and we, as a Christian, practice prayer, isn't that talking to someone who has died?

———·———

Accessing the Realms of Heaven

A tremendous privilege we share in this time in history is the ability to access the realms of Heaven with ease. Many of us were taught that Heaven is only for after we die. Heaven is much more than a final destination on a journey but also can be a vital aspect of that journey.

What I am about to share is vital in progressing in the various Courts of Heaven. We can access the Mercy Court in the Heavenly realm while fully planted here on the earth, but to maximize our endeavors in the Courts of Heaven, we need to learn how to operate FROM Heaven.

In teaching on accessing the realms of Heaven, I often point out some simple facts. If you were to tell me you were a citizen of a particular town, but you could tell me little of it from your personal experience, I would have a tendency to doubt the authenticity of your citizenship. I am a citizen of a small town in central North Carolina. I am familiar with the location of the city hall, police station, hospital, local county courthouse, Sheriff's Department, and much more. I know where many sporting events will be held. I know where the parks are. I know many of the stores and restaurants. I am familiar with this small town. Yet, if I were to ask the average believer what they can describe of Heaven from personal experience, the answer will likely be nothing. They have no personal experience of Heaven that they can relate to me. It does not have to be like that.

In Matthew 3, Jesus informed us that the Kingdom of Heaven was at hand. We could say, "The Kingdom of Heaven is as close as our hand." Hold our hand up in front of our nose as close as we could. Do not touch our nose. Heaven is closer to us than that. It is not far, far away up in the sky. It is not "over yonder" as some old hymns describe. It is a very present reality separated from us by a very thin membrane—and we can access it by faith. It is very simple.

When Jesus was baptized in the River Jordan, as He came up out of the water IMMEDIATELY the heavens were opened. He both saw (a dove) and heard (a voice coming from Heaven). This one act of Jesus restored our ability to access Heaven. We can experience open heavens over our life. We don't have to wait. We can live conscious of the realm of Heaven and live out of that reality!

Everything we do as believers we must do by faith. Accessing the realms of Heaven is done the same way.

Prophetic acts can create realities for us. It is the same with this. We can visualize stepping from one room into another easily. It is like stepping from one place to another. To learn to access the realms of Heaven, we will follow the same pattern.

Stand up from where we are now and prepare to work with me. We can experience the realms of Heaven right now! We don't have to wait until we are dressed up in a long box at the local funeral home or decorating an urn. We can experience Heaven while we are alive! Remember, we enter the Kingdom as a child.

Quiet ourselves down. Turn off distracting background noises if possible. Prepare to relax and focus. Now, say this with me:

Father, I would like to access the realms of Heaven today, so right now, by faith, I take a step into the realms of Heaven. [As we say that, take a step forward.] Imagine we are going from one place to another in a single step. Once we have done so, pay attention to what we see and hear. We may see very bright lights; we may see a river, a pastoral scene, a garden—any number of things. Right now, we are experiencing a taste of Heaven. We will notice the peace that pervades the atmosphere of Heaven. We might notice the air seems electric with life. The testimonies I've heard are always amazing and beautiful to hear.

Now spend a few minutes in this place. Remember, Jesus said that to enter the Kingdom we must come as a little child. I often coach people to imagine ourselves as an 8-year-old with what we are seeing. What would an 8-year-old do? He or she would be inquisitive and ask, "What is this? What does that do? Where does that go? Can I go here?" If a child saw a river or a lake, what would that child want to do? Most would want to jump in the water.

The variety is infinite. The colors—amazing! The sounds are so beautiful. We can learn to do this on a regular basis. When we access the realms of Heaven, we are home. We were made to experience the beauty that is Heaven.

The reason learning to access the realms of Heaven is crucial to engaging the Courts of Heaven is that much of what we do is done FROM Heaven. We need to learn to engage Heaven and work from it.

Many people tell me they can't "see" visually in the spirit. Often, they are discounting the ability they do have. They may be discounting their "knower." Every believer has a "knower" at work within them. This "knower" who is Holy Spirit at work within us helps us perceive things. Whether something is good or evil, He works to guide us more than we may have realized. Most navies that have submarines have a device known as sonar. Sonar gives a submarine "eyes" to see what is in their vicinity. They can detect what the object is by the ping emitted by the sonar. They can determine the distance to the object and if it is another submarine. They can even identify what class of submarine it might be.

Sonar is invaluable in this setting, but a video camera would be rather useless underwater.

The military has a similar device for above ground situations known as radar. It functions in much the same manner. If a pilot were flying through thick cloud cover, the pilot would need to know what is in his path. Radar becomes his eyes.

Some people function visually. They often see what amounts to pictures or video images when they "see" in the spirit. They may see more detail. Yet one operating by his or her "knower" (their spiritual radar or sonar) can be just as effective as a seer. If we operate more like sonar or radar, don't discount what we "see" in that manner. It is how I function, and I have been doing this type of work for many years.

I can often detect where an angel is in the room (or if it is one of the men or women in white linen and not an angel). I can often detect how many are present and whether they have something they are to give to someone. I can detect any number of things and even though it is not "visual" it is still "seeing." It will set our mind at ease when we understand that operating by our knower is just as valid as any other type of vision. It will help us to realize we have been seeing much more than we know and we may know much more than some who only see.

———·———

Evil Timelines

Following the Coastal Carolina Conference, Adina, Robert, Jody, and I underwent severe physical attacks. We had stayed an additional 3 days at an AirBNB near the beach. Several strategies of the enemy were put into play one after another. I won't discuss all of those at this point, just the most pertinent one where Lydia instructed us on *Understanding Evil Timelines.*

We had been seeking answers concerning what we had been experiencing and thoughts came and were expressed that, 'Ron and Adina are suffering from a physical ailment with which they are not in agreement with, and they do not have the fear of it. They will recover. However (and here's the radical thought), we need to declare a timeline shift—the shift over to the Godly timeline, where Ron & Adina never got sick—the spiritual timeline in the spirit, which is the true timeline, not the fake.

This line of thought was the result of a dream my Executive Assistant had over the weekend. She described the dream.

> *Last night, several times in the night, I had this dream. I saw two images of Ron. The two Ron's I saw were identical copies of each other and they were standing nearby each other, but one was elevated. I worked this dream through with Holy Spirit. As I pondered it to this point, I believe He's showing that there is another timeline in play here, and we can invite the true timeline in since it's the truth, align with the truth, and speak that over Ron and Adina.*

She and the intercessors did some prayer work earlier related to this but did not feel it was complete. More information was needed. Describing what she sensed about that scenario, she said, "It's almost like this; when the four of us left and went to that condo that wasn't very happy, we stepped into a weird portal that took this alternative timeline and ran with it. We had to close the gate, close the door to that. I don't think it's finished."

The Skate Key

She continued, "The other dream I had, and I'm not sure it's connected, but I feel like it is. I had this thought sometime in the night. I was suddenly thinking about a skate key. In the morning, I even had to ask Lawrence if he even remembered this object after decades of not ever thinking about a skate key. I had the thought that I had been given something called a skate key (for use with our old-fashioned roller skates).

"Do we remember back in the day? Metal skates were adjustable. We put the skate on our foot, but then we had to lock it using the key, so it would fit us. Everybody always said, "Don't lose the skate key! We had it on a shoestring tied around and hanging from our neck because we needed it every now and then because the skates would loosen as we skated. I probably had this when I was in the first grade.

"I was given a skate key and I kept thinking about a skate key all night long. Something had been awarded that was a key. Jesus owns all the keys—so, it came from Him. I had a key, and it was to skate, but I had to lock it on and keep it locked. In other words, we must lock in! We must focus if we're going to receive the thing that's going to cause us to skate. I think the skate analogy is just moving forward at a faster accelerated pace. I praise the Lord for that, and I do think that's happening because I'm getting some revelatory flow on some things.

"Back to this timeline issue.

"As a son of God, I step into the Business Complex of Heaven requesting in the name of Jesus to meet with Lydia."

Understanding Evil Timelines

Satan attempts to change times and laws. This is true with the fabric of time and his desire to be able to create as the Father does. The Creator creates. We must remember, there is no end to the lust that Satan has for the attributes of God, the attributes of Yahweh, the attributes of the Most High. This has gotten him in trouble, and it will eventually result in his destruction. Nevertheless, before us now is the understanding of his attempt at capturing time.

It's true. Witchcraft is used in this, even incantations from of old. And when I say old, I mean, ancient, I mean pre-flood. I mean the knowledge of the Counsels of Heaven of which Satan had knowledge of at that time, but for which, when he corrupted his being, he was cast down.

Nevertheless, being cast out doesn't mean he lost some of the knowledge that he carried—that his former self carried. However, his former self—it was not his current self in that moment. His knowledge was corrupt. He had knowledge, but it was corrupted knowledge. He had corrupted it by the corruption of his own being. (This sounds like a circular argument, but we'll find a pathway in it.)

Therefore, he attempts to bring time under his dominion. And the creation of another timeline is his attempt. We'll notice that the corrupt timeline is only an attempt. **It can be reversed by the sons of God,**

through the glory portals of Heaven. And the sons of God are learning to do this. The reversal of corrupt or false (we may call them evil timelines) is first to see them in our vision. That's what we were shown.

What was seen was Ron's realm. Then we were shown another "Ron's realm" and it appeared an identical copy. Yet, there was no combination of the two, they were separated.

Heaven's help is to adjust the timeline back to the original—to the Word of God, to the Word of the Living God. Evil attempts to corrupt the Word. Our sense of this was correct. To progress to the next step, our understanding must catch up with what our spirit knows, and that is the part I'm playing. [That was the part Lydia was playing for us.]

Our soul is going to want to know why, but I want to show us the reconciliation of the time and where it malfunctioned due to corrupt beings and agents of darkness. I am not going to show us the humans that were used to accomplish this because there are many, but just know that the deception Satan pulls on humanity is for the purpose of using them for his gain, which is to corrupt all things for:

Satan can have dominion over corruption and things that are corrupted, but he cannot have dominion over light and things that are righteous.

Satan will take that which is righteous and attempt to corrupt it, to bring about his will over that human. For the human agents of darkness, this is their pit, this is their temptation to sin, which has trapped them in deception.

Some of these will come out. Some of these will not, because their will has chosen their preference and their conscience has been seared. While I will use the words incantation and witchcraft, we may know that there are many voices in this hour set against the Glory of God; but Ron has determined to be the releaser of The Glory and the agents of darkness tremble. When I say tremble, they don't have an answer for this. Therefore, they must stop the portal that it's coming through. If coming through Ron's portal, they seek to shut it down. Do we see how this is not a personal vendetta against Ron? It is a generalized fear of light and glory through God's timeline fabric.

Paths can be smooth and made without wrinkle. It's the wrinkle that is the issue. It's the problem. *The wrinkle is the point of the two timelines*, because a wrinkle comes when we have an overlay of fabric. It's a wrinkle—an aberration in the fabric. It layers one on another. The need is to *smooth, straighten, and stretch out* the timeline fabric with the release of angels to do this and with the verdicts of courts to release for the destruction the other timeline. These go hand in hand.

The destruction of the other timeline needs a verdict of the Just Judge. We are seeking a verdict of destruction of the false timeline.

This is an ownership issue of one's timeline fabric. I say "timeline fabric" because it's not a *line*—it's a fabric. Courts exist for these verdicts, for the overturning of the false timeline like a false verdict from Courts of Hell.

And yet, it also involves a false ownership as the false verdict attempts to elicit an ownership over what the corruption has created, the corrupt timeline. The false verdicts create false ownership over a false creation and the illusion of a timeline. I say illusion, yet I only use that word because an illusion is a copy of the real. Yet, an illusion can be manipulated to one's own end that the incantation has for which the thing or condition has been named. So yes, I'll use the word "spell" if we are thinking that is what this is, don't let these words ruffle us. They are simply the corruption of prayer.

Don't let them ruffle us because they are simply the corruption of prayer—actually, the corruption of the two-way communication of prayer and revelation.

Spells and incantations are simply the corruption of the two-way communication of prayer and revelation.

Remember, we have told us over and over how important our voices are. There's one proof of this.

Agents of darkness operate with their voices all the time. Where are God's sons are to operate likewise in like manner, but in more power?

---

*This should be a wakeup call
to the sons of God.*

I will say this, this is also why there are muzzles upon the male portion of the sons of God. These muzzles on the male portion of the sons of God are wicked and almost at a fullness where the judgment of God will fall.

---

*There are more of the female portion
of the sons of God crying out.*

And what is their cry? **Their cry is for their offspring.**

---

*When the sons of God begin
to cry out for their offspring,
that the muzzles will break apart!*

For this is righteousness and light; that the offspring of the sons of God be contended for by the sons of God, that portion, which is male, not *just* female. But when the portion that is male and the portion that is female cry out together to our God for the deliverance of the offspring which carry His likeness and to whom will be granted the rulership of the King, the combination of Righteous Rule will break forth.

At a recent conference, we prayed for the men and prayed that the shackles be broken asunder and removed, even for the slavery of the mouth.

The slavery of the mouth is at work on the male portion of the sons of God.

Not *all* sickness is a result of evil timelines. There is a myriad of reasonings behind this corruption of flesh. And I'm highlighting to us now, a segment of the corruption.

Some have been involved in corrupted timelines.

What is needed?

Lydia began explaining the strategy to handle the timeline issue:

- A verdict in the Appellate Court for the overturning of the false verdict regarding timelines is needed.
- A subsequent verdict that all false ownership claims on false timelines be overturned.
- We will need to request a destruction by fire of the ungodly timeline.
- We will need to request angelic activity for the smoothing of the timeline.

- We will need to appear in the Court of Reclamation to receive back what has been stolen due to the divergence that took place[58];
- We will need to come into agreement verbally. The individual for which the case is taking place—our client—would need to verbally receive back into their realm, their Father's timeline of fabric. **They would need to make an agreement with it.**
- They would need to enforce the agreement from their realm, by their belief. Yes, in faith that there has been a change, like a railroad track where we pull the lever and the track changed from one track to another track.
    - This is a helpful visual to combat the lie of Satan, about his ability to keep us in an alternative, evil timeline.
- We need our mouth.
- We need our staunch firm stance to declare we will only walk in and live and move and have our being through the Father's righteous timeline and that every timeline divergence is cursed by God, in Jesus' name.

Hollywood has portrayed all of this stuff before the sons and daughters of God, and some are catching onto

---

[58] Always, when accessing the Court of Reclamations, request information from the court as to what you may ask for in reclamation.

this. There's a current TV series with the character called Loki and it's about divergent timelines.

We wanted to take this to the Father, and we needed Lydia's help. We're going to enforce this as sons of God.

> *Father, we request to enter the Court of Appeals—the Appellate Court of Heaven, in the name of Jesus. We enter in as an advocate on Ron Horner's behalf. I enter in as an advocate on Adina Horner's behalf. I enter in as an advocate on Robert Woeger's behalf and on Jody Woeger's behalf, these four. I am seeking a reversal and an overturning of a false verdict from the Courts of Hell for these four regarding an alternative evil and corrupt timeline instituted by witchcraft, occultic incantations, and spells.*
>
> *I am requesting the overturning of this by the blood of Jesus and the superior court verdict of this court.*
>
> *I simply repent on behalf of Your sons, both male and female, Father; where we have not operated with gratefulness of the timeline You've given us; the time fabric You've given us; where we've been ignorant of the time fabric that You've given; where we've been ignorant of Satan's evil; where we have been ignorant of his lies; where we have not sought revelation about these things that we might bring them to You quickly. I repent for that. I confess it as sin on all our behalf (mine included)*

in the name of Jesus. I ask, Father, that You would cover this with the blood of Your Son, Jesus.

I also request in Your Appellate Court, the overturning and cancellation of the false timeline and the ownership of that timeline. I ask that it would be overruled and overturned, and that the ownership of the timeline of these people—these four and their timeline fabric would be given to the Lord Jesus Christ.

I ask for the complete destruction by fire of every evil, corrupt wrinkle and overlay of false evil timelines and I request the verdict of this court to affect the re-entrance of and the remaining upon the smooth timeline fabric of the Father's time for these four, as written by the Word of God before the foundation of the earth and as written in the Books of Heaven and as linked to their destiny as sons of God.

I request angelic assistance for each of these to receive a smoothing of timeline fabric so that it will be without wrinkle.

I also request authorization to move to the Court of Reclamation as the evil and corrupt timeline is destroyed.

I request an alignment in these individuals, spirit realm, soul realm, and body realm to supernaturally be made whole, to supernaturally *be aligned so that the perfection of body healing, soul trauma, and spirit understanding would be returned to them in the twinkling of an eye.*

I request this in Jesus' name.

We received the verdict which came easily and quickly because Satan had not had time to trade on this evil timeline. It had not been traded on. It had been in existence, but not traded on.

We, as sons, must be careful with this type of court case, because we also may need to request the overturning—the severing of any trade on that timeline—that evil, corrupt timeline.

If it is traded upon, it has become a trading floor. These have not, but that's a distinct possibility. This trading floor is evil. It is created as an evil trading floor off the evil timeline and we would need to deal with that.

If it had been traded on, then we would need to have the cancellation of the evil trading floor and all evil trades. It is as easy as that. That would be the third step.

We heard from the court about this where they said that those who are suffering in an evil timeline that has evil trading floors linked to it, the result of that—is we see is the life source being stolen from that person—the life force, the life energy, the life of the person, begins to drain from the flesh and it drains to the point where their spirit leaves their natural body, because Satan is after their spirit to put the spirit in enslavement.

We went to the Court of Reclamations and petitioned:

Father, I ask in the name of Jesus, to enter your Court of Reclamations on behalf and as an advocate on behalf of Ron Horner, Adina Horner, Robert Woeger, and Jody Woeger, and request, a reclamation and restitution. I request that the Council of this Court would come forth, so that I can know what to request by way of restitution.

I request a return from the moment of the time divergence until now, which is the moment of revelation of what the thief has stolen, be returned to these four, seven-fold in their body, in their soul and in their spirit, health returned robustly seven-fold, trauma, anything removed from the soul that—despair be turned to gladness, that that hopelessness turn to faith achieved, that isolation turn to community connection; that all the God-given ability to operate from revelation that results in the work of their hands and the deeds of the mouth (these were stolen) that these be returned seven-fold. I request these, in the name of Jesus.

We were instructed to view what we were asking for as the jewels of the stones of the City, speaking of the stones in the New Jerusalem. The New Jerusalem is built on them. The stones of the city are jasper, pearl, onyx, and lapis. We requested these stones be returned as they had been stolen from the sons of God. We prayed:

I am requesting in the Court of Reclamations for an amendment where Satan's kingdom would suffer harm, where Satan's kingdom would suffer plunder, where angels would be released to plunder the enemy and bring back more than what was lost just as David did at Ziklag. He received back more than what was stolen because the enemy's camp was plundered. We request this in the name of Jesus.

I also request the counsel of this court for the number of days one has been laid low to be added to their length of days in Jesus' name.

This concludes my court case. I thank you, Father, that You hear these things and rule with justice and righteousness from Your Throne. Hallelujah.

The Court brought another issue to our attention. The Court wanted to know, "Do we want to request in this plundering of Satan's kingdom, regarding those individuals who are deceived, who operate through the deception of darkness where their own lips cast incantations and spells, would it be our choice to request a salvation and redemption encounter for those humans locked in their despair?"

We replied that we would and prayed accordingly:

Yes, we would. We would request that in the name of Jesus Christ.

We agree with the angel of the Lord visiting these five persons.

Alright. We add our faith to this, that sons of God will see the light. They will know His love, and they will feel their freedom from shackles and chains. In Jesus name. Hallelujah. Amen.

———·———

Description

Having written about a radical change to the deliverance modalities common in the charismatic/Pentecostal streams of the Body of Christ, Dr. Ron M. Horner continues to unpack helpful information in how to effectively deal with the concept of Lingering Human Spirits. This book is not an introductory book but is for those who are working in this modality. It explores vital information related to this subject and will help us become more effective as we minister this redemptive work to those who have yet to make the transition to Heaven and the destiny that awaits them.

About the Author

Dr. Ron Horner is an apostolic teacher specializing in the Courts of Heaven. He has written over twenty books on the Courts of Heaven, engaging Heaven, working with angels, or living from revelation.

He currently trains people in engaging the Courts of Heaven in a weekly online teaching session. You can register to participate and discover more about the Courts of Heaven prayer paradigm from his various websites, classes, products, and services found here:

www.ronhorner.com

_____ · _____

Other Books by Dr. Ron M. Horner

Building Your Business from Heaven Down

Building Your Business from Heaven Down 2.0

Building Your Business with the Blueprint of Heaven

Commissioning Angels – Volume 1

Cooperating with The Glory

Courts of Heaven Process Charts

Dealing with Trusts & Consequential Liens from the Courts of Heaven

Engaging Angels in the Realms of Heaven

Engaging Heaven for Revelation – Volume 1

Engaging Heaven for Revelation – Volume 2

Engaging Heaven for Trade

Engaging the Courts for Ownership & Order

Engaging the Courts for Your City (*Paperback, Leader's Guide & Workbook*)

Engaging the Courts of Healing & the Healing Garden

Engaging the Courts of Heaven

Engaging the Help Desk of the Courts of Heaven

Engaging the Mercy Court of Heaven

Four Keys to Dismantling Accusations

Freedom from Mithraism

Kingdom Dynamics – Volume 1

Kingdom Dynamics – Volume 2

Let's Get it Right!

Lingering Human Spirits

Lingering Human Spirits – Volume 2

Living Spirit Forward

Overcoming the False Verdicts of Freemasonry

Overcoming Verdicts from the Courts of Hell

Releasing Bonds from the Courts of Heaven

Unlocking Spiritual Seeing

SPANISH

Cómo Proceder en la Corte Celestial de Misericordia

Las Cuatro Llaves para Anular las Acusaciones

Liberando Bonos en las Cortes Celestiales

Liberando Su Visión Espiritual

Sea Libre del Mitraísmo

Tablas de Proceso de la Cortes del Cielo

Viviendo desde el Espíritu

www.ingramcontent.com/pod-product-compliance
Lightning Source LLC
Chambersburg PA
CBHW030814190426
43197CB00035B/257